The Crooked Scythe

George Ewart Evans

THE CROOKED SCYTHE

An anthology of oral history

Edited and with drawings by

DAVID GENTLEMAN

faber and faber

First published in 1993
by Faber and Faber Limited
3 Queen Square London WC1N 3AU
This paperback edition first published in 1994

Photoset by Parker Typesetting Service, Leicester
Printed in England by Clays Ltd, St Ives Plc

A CIP record for this book is available from the British Library

ISBN 0–571–17194–X

2 4 6 8 10 9 7 5 3 1

Then to the Plough, (the Common-wealth)
Next to your Flailes, your Fanes, your Fatts;
Then to the Maids with Wheaten Hats:
To the rough Sickle, and crookt Sythe,
Drink, frollick, boyes, till all be blythe.

Robert Herrick, from *The Hock-cart or Harvest Home*

CONTENTS

EDITORIAL NOTE The list of books by George Ewart Evans from which the extracts
in *The Crooked Scythe* are taken appears on page 199. In the text square brackets or
ellipsis [. . .] show where cuts have been made. Within extracts an extra line of space
between passages indicates that the published text has been shortened. Page
references to the original book are given for each extract at the end of the anthology.
The headlines above extracts have been provided by the editor. Footnotes are the
author's unless shown otherwise. The names in SMALL CAPITALS at the end of
many passages are those of Mr Evans's informants, the texts his transcription of their
spoken words.

INTRODUCTION

Helmingham

I first met George Ewart Evans in the spring of 1966, when he was living with his wife, Florence, in School House in Helmingham, a trim Suffolk village still clearly under the wing of Helmingham Hall. I'd gone to spend a few weeks there in order to make some drawings for his third book, *The Pattern Under the Plough*. This work involved many delightful expeditions. George would take me in his Mini to see things he'd written about – houses, farms, villages, bits of landscape, people he knew – and later I would go back on my own and draw them. This was a congenial task. In between drawings, I would return to School House for good simple meals made by Florence, which always included her own home-made bread. From time to time on our expeditions George and I would go to a pub. Florence, who was a Quaker and didn't like pubs, never came with us, but their youngest daughter, Sue, sometimes did. She was lively and unpredictable, and I was much attracted to her. In due course we got married.

One of the people George took me to meet on that first Helmingham visit was Sam Friend, the Suffolk horseman who is, after Robert and Prissy Savage of Blaxhall, the most vividly drawn individual in his books. While Sam gave us tea in his small living-room, I drew the scene: the old man in his heavy corduroy jacket, and some curious details like his plaited leather belt and the fine earthenware teapot he had brought back from Burton upon Trent, where one autumn many years before he had gone to work in the maltings.

There were many other such visits: to nearby villages, like Brandeston, to see Hector Moore's forge, and Framsden, where there was a post-mill; to the Haddiscoe marshes where the Pettingill family lived in a lonely and isolated farmhouse; to some abandoned maltings at Bungay, where the maltsters' big wooden shovels and metal rakes were still lying about. Later on, some of the expeditions were further afield: to Norwich cattle market, for example, to Heveningham Hall, where standing in a field was an old timber-jim, a heavy two-wheeled cart under which could be slung a whole tree-trunk, and to Blaxhall, where we had a glass of beer in the Ship Inn. And many years later, when he was writing his autobiography *The Strength of the Hills*, we went to his Welsh valley birthplace in Abercynon, where we visited Penywaun, the remote farm where as a boy George had delivered groceries in a pony and trap; we saw the dry-stone wall where George and his friends had leant and wondered what to do in the Depression; and we climbed the bracken-covered hills over which the lines of black-clothed miners had walked after the Senghenydd pit disaster.

For me, such visits were given an edge by the need to find interesting things to draw – however enjoyable, they were also work. But there were many other pleasant occasions with no such practical task in mind: family picnics on the beach at Southwold or the shingle at Dunwich; a visit to Barsham Fair. I particularly remember one afternoon some fifteen years ago when George and Florence helped Sue and me and our own young children to prepare, level, rake and sow with grass and clover seed the neglected patch of land behind the Suffolk cottage we had recently bought; finally rolling it and planting it all with stakes, each with a fluttering streamer of bright metal foil glittering at the top, to keep the birds off the new seed.

George was born in 1909 in Abercynon, a mining village in the Cynon valley north of Cardiff. He was one of a family of eleven. His parents, who spoke Welsh, ran a modest grocery business; as a boy, George made the delivery round by pony and trap to the outlying farms, until the coal strike of 1924–5 forced his parents out of business. George went to the nearby grammar school at Mountain Ash, where he was good at rugby and running – he ran professionally for a while – and went on to read classics at Cardiff University. He then found himself with no job, no prospects, and no ambitions apart from a fixed resolve to write. He had an unsuccessful shot at finding work in London, followed by a period of near despair back in Abercynon, when he found some peace of mind mending boots; but he was eventually taken on as a teacher, not of classics but of physical training, at the first Village College at Sawston, near Cambridge. There he met and married his fellow teacher Florence Knappett, and started a family. He served in the RAF during the war, maintaining wireless equipment. After the Sawston house burned down, he moved first to north London and then in 1947 to the remote Suffolk village of Blaxhall. While Florence taught in the village school and, in what was then an unusual reversal of the conventional roles, earned most of the family's income, George looked after the young children and really began to write in earnest. He wrote poetry and stories, film scripts for children, and radio scripts for the BBC. And then in the early fifties, still uncertain where his true interest lay, he sat down and wrote a book on the subject he knew most about: Blaxhall and the lives of his neighbours there. This remarkable book, *Ask the Fellows Who Cut the Hay*, was rejected by a string of publishers, but in 1956 Faber and Faber published it, and in due course the ten other related books which George was to write over the next thirty years.

The family lived fairly simply, even frugally, because for a long time they had very little money – certainly they had none to spare when the four children were young. The children went to a Quaker boarding-school: Florence's being a Quaker helped here, as they were paid for by the Society of Friends. But for a long time George could not afford to buy a car, and family outings with the young children were by bus or on bicycles. There were no family holidays.

George and Florence remained in Suffolk while their children grew up, the family home following Florence's posts as headmistress from Blaxhall to Needham Market and then to Helmingham. Apart from occasional visits, George never returned to live in Wales, though he sometimes wanted to. Even when the children had left home and Florence had retired from teaching, they stayed on in East Anglia, settling down eventually in a cottage in Brooke, the small Norfolk village where he went on writing. By then his work had become widely known; most of his books remained in print, many in paperback, and his work had also become influential and respected in the academic world which had earlier looked on it with some suspicion.

Brooke is a pretty village not far from Norwich, where many of its inhabitants now work; but George found it gentrified and unreal, feeling that it had become a dormitory suburb, and he hankered for Suffolk or Wales. None the less, he wrote seven of his books there, sitting at a wooden desk surrounded by books, near a tall filing-cabinet full of letters and tapes, with a bottle of sherry for visitors standing on the floor beside it. One window looked on to his hedge, the other on to a small lawn with a Portuguese laurel tree and the shallow Brooke mere beyond it; at the back of the cottage was a long garden shaded by apple trees. George was a good gardener and the place always looked trim and abundant until finally, when he became ill, the heavy garden work got too much for him. But he was still fruitfully at work writing almost to the end of his days: *Spoken History* was published the year before he died.

Florence and he were also good and patient grandparents. George had the same happy ability to make a small child feel at ease as he had with his 'informants', the rather stiff word he used for the people he recorded on tape, and he recorded the voices of the grandchildren very early in their lives. He enjoyed playing back to us these and other favourite tapes. Even then, many of the people he had recorded were very old; now, of course, they have almost all vanished.

George was in his mid-fifties when I first saw him, but he seemed younger: upright and vigorous, with an open and friendly manner and a clear, piercing gaze. He looked the part of a countryman, in a tweed jacket, a hat also of tweed, drill trousers, and stout brown shoes. As I grew to know him, I discovered that he was sympathetic and generous with help and encouragement. He was intelligent and shrewd; his judgements, though seldom sharply expressed, were acute and penetrating. He was humorous, balanced and rational. In conversation he was tolerant and unassertive, but it was soon clear that he held independent views with firmness and conviction.

Most of these beliefs and opinions are quite clear from reading the books; conversation with him simply confirmed them. Politically he was consistently and vigorously on the left, a conviction that grew from his Welsh valley childhood and was only strengthened by time. He also had a Welshman's unshakeable faith in the importance of education. He admired the old Reithian BBC, especially the Third Programme, as a powerful educational institution; the BBC broadcast several memorable programmes of his tapes. He thought that the advent of commercial television was the single most destructive influence on the country's culture. He was ambivalent about the country gentry, impressed by them but able to see that their control over a 'closed' village like Helmingham had been both benevolent and oppressive. He was an atheist; yet when exploring an old church he had a respect not only for its architecture but for its links with past generations in whose lives it had played an important part. He was half amused, half exasperated by the church's efforts to shore up its dwindling or terminal position in rural society.

His attitude to moral questions was practical and without bigotry, and he was sensible and matter-of-fact in speaking or writing about sex. But he could be very reticent: his courtship and marriage are only briefly touched on in *The Strength of the Hills*; he evidently thought this too personal a matter even to write about. Perhaps he was right to be reticent; certainly it was in character. But his brief account of a fleeting wartime encounter with a Scottish WAAF girl is far more vivid. He was more interested in Jung and the collective unconscious than in Freudian theory, which he thought had taken the place of religious belief. What he did believe in was the ability of people, whether educated or not, to understand for themselves and communicate the realities of their own lives; and he thought the most important of these realities was their work. These are the convictions that sustained him and are expressed throughout the books.

But despite the optimistic nature of his views, there was a down side to his personality. He was prey, now and then, to the 'black dog' – the periods of gloom and despair that are the price people occasionally pay for working alone. He wrote about them only in his unpublished diaries. These depressions, partly the result of difficult living circumstances, were worst while he was living in north London just after the war, when the children were very young. Later on, when the family had moved to Blaxhall, the depressions eased, but he still had some serious practical problems to contend with. In the fifties he contracted tuberculosis; and, paradoxically for someone with such an acute ear for the way people speak, he became deaf enough to need a hearing-aid. But I never knew him to grumble.

As a writer he led rather an isolated existence. Though he had taught briefly as a young man, he never returned to academic life: working on his own, as an outsider, free of institutional loyalties and responsibilities, was essential for him. It allowed him to be independent and inquiring: *all* his work and thinking could be directed at the things that most interested him. But this independence, however invigorating, had its drawbacks. Without a body of like-minded individuals to count on for reassurance and support, he could feel out of touch, ignored, and even occasionally scorned. The case he makes in the books for oral or spoken history as a serious discipline was made at first in the face of a good deal of scorn for the whole subject.

But while he may have felt out of the mainstream in certain ways, George was sustained over his writing life by several long-standing friendships. He kept up a correspondence with Robert Graves over many years; and a friendship that was particularly important to him was with the writer David Thomson – another Celt – and his wife Martina. In the fifties and early sixties David was working at the BBC, and he produced several radio programmes built round George's tapes: one on the folklore of the hare, another on working in the Burton maltings. Until then I'd never heard of George, but these programmes made a great impression on me: they were original, full of substance, reality and beauty. The association led in turn to their jointly written book *The Leaping Hare*, in which the Irish voices that David knew are joined with the mainly East Anglian ones of the other books.

The scope of George's work is complex and hard to define. His books might seem on the surface to be simply about two subjects: the countryside, and the past. Much in them is indeed remembered: old people talking clearly and vividly about how things were, in their recurrent phrase, 'at that time of day' – that is, when they were younger. Certainly one can enjoy the books in a spirit of nostalgia, and take pleasure in the charm of the rural subject matter. But George was too clear-headed and too objective for nostalgia, and one quickly finds out – as he did – that the lives and times he recorded were far too hard for anyone with any humanity to wish them back. Rather, he used the past as a way to understand the present. And his examples have not dated or lost their relevance. For example, when I first read *The Strength of the Hills*, its account of the harsh recession of the thirties seemed as remote from our own times as Dickens or Mayhew. But now, with another long recession in full swing, his account seems fresh, true and relevant.

George's understanding was underpinned by his own keen sense of history, which was objective and radical: an individual view, soundly based on readings ranging from nineteenth-century farming textbooks back to the sixteenth-century farming poet Thomas Tusser, and to Chaucer and Virgil's *Georgics*. This makes it hard to find a label, a category, for him: he was not writing about simple, identifiable subjects like 'folklore' or 'the countryside' or 'farming methods' or even 'social history', but about something more complicated, more comprehensive and more poetic: what he had seen happening in his own lifetime to a long-established tradition.

In this he was by no means a detached observer, but an active participant. Thus, when he noticed some of the Blaxhall children turning blue, he not only traced the cause to contamination of the village well by nitrates from farm fertilizers, but also managed to get piped water laid on for the village. Worried about how heavy farm machinery was damaging the fragile soil structure, he joined the early ecological society Men of the Earth. He was concerned about an immediate local predicament, long before ecology and the environment became universal preoccupations, so his books touch on questions that have grown more, not less, important as time passes: questions about how we live, and whether we are leaving things better or worse than we found them, and what future our children can look forward to. His achievement was to set these minority, even esoteric, concerns in a credible historic context, to flesh them out with personal experience, and to gain a wide audience for them.

The thread which binds the books together is George's technique of using a tape-recorder to enable people to describe their lives and their work in their own words. Despite his own deafness, he became most skilful with the tape-recorder. He was careful not to hurry or try to lead the conversation; it had to take its own course, in several sessions if need be. He found out that what he did not expect to hear could be more interesting than his preconceived expectations. It was important that there should be genuine trust on both sides. He also transcribed the tapes with skill and sensitivity, particularly in the difficult matter of orthography and spelling of a Suffolk usage or accent – he was able accurately to transcribe old usages like *bo'* or *bor* (boy), *yeh* or *yeah* (yes) without the transcription looking patronizing or folksy. His skill as a historian and his sympathetic understanding allowed him first to elicit and then to give coherence to this fascinating raw material, something to which no one had previously paid any attention.

Rereading the books now, two things strike me most vividly. The first is the freshness and authenticity of the transcribed speech of his informants – the vigour and truth of their recorded voices. Language like this is extremely hard to imagine or imitate: the attempt can easily sound embarrassing. Even George's own shots at re-creating vernacular speech, as in the short stories about the Norfolk character Acky, don't really have the same ring of truth as his transcriptions of the real thing.

The second striking aspect is the artistry with which the accounts have been elicited and selected. Finding the right person to talk to is important; but tape-recording someone talking is like taking a photograph. it will certainly provide a true record of some sort, but not necessarily an interesting or significant one. What is remarkable in these recordings is George's skill, patience and evident sympathy in drawing out people's memories and feelings. He knew how to persuade people – even those who, poor and occasionally illiterate, might easily have been overlooked or thought inarticulate – to reveal themselves, their memories, ideas and conclusions, candidly and expressively. This is difficult to do well. George succeeded because he was obviously an honest and decent person with whom they could feel in sympathy. He was neither impatient nor superior, nor was he an inquisitive and ignorant outsider; as the village schoolmistress's husband, albeit without any apparent job, he belonged to the local community as surely as they did themselves.

George's informants fall into several distinct groups. In the first are his immediate close friends and neighbours, like Robert and Prissy Savage at Blaxhall. Next come a more widely scattered range of friends: horsemen, smiths, saddlers and other craftsmen, people he sought out or had been directed to by other friends. And third are the people who sought *him* out – who came, for example, to his courses of lectures on local history for the Workers Educational Association out of interest in the subject, and then ended up being interviewed and recorded in their own turn.

The other essential element in George's work is its significant timing: the historical watershed at which these interviews took place. He was recording experience of a mainly rural way of life that had, as he convincingly argues, continued little changed for centuries, even millennia, just when it was on the point of vanishing: at the moment, that is, when its age-old dependence on animal power finally switched to reliance on machinery. George called the old order 'the prior culture'. What he did, with insight and clarity, was to set the skills and beauties of this prior culture – the way, for instance, to plough a field *perfectly*, or to persuade an unwilling horse to do what one wanted – side by side with the harshness of the toil, the meagreness of the reward, and the rigidity of the social structures, that were inseparable from them. He has preserved these realities for us through the living voices of the people who spoke to him, neither as grumbles about hard times nor as sentimental nostalgia, but as compelling accounts of how things were by people who knew.

This search for reality, for the disappearing truth, sometimes led him away from historians' accepted documentary sources into uncharted waters: into investigating the hay trade, for instance, which had fuelled horses (and thus the army) as surely as petrol fuels our cars, or the Suffolk farm labourers' annual migration after the harvest to Burton upon Trent for the heavy seasonal work in the maltings there. This migration was significant historically, yet its only documentary record – in the maltsters' ledgers – was being casually thrown out and lost even as George was making his recordings.

In making this selection of George's writings, I have generally chosen extracts from the recorded interviews – his raw material – and tended to avoid his commentary and his theoretical summing up. This is not because it is dull – it is interesting and convincing – but because his commentary is hard to take out of its context: it is better read alongside the preceding material than separated from it. I've chosen the interviews for their individual interest and to show the wide range of people he was friendly with: horsemen, farm-workers, hay-traders, auctioneers, his village neighbours, miners, fishermen and seamen, and some remarkable women.

The underlying preoccupation in all George's books is with people and change. He knew that change, with its good aspects and bad, was inevitable, and he viewed it dispassionately. The Suffolk of his early books has gone on changing since he wrote: brought nearer to London by faster roads, its small towns bypassed and pedestrianized, its railways pruned, its neglected and tumbledown cottages done up, its great houses sold to syndicates, its patchwork of small hedged fields transformed into an open prairie landscape, its busy farms worked by one or two solitary mechanics, its older generation dead. Now that George too, like his informants, is dead, I miss not only his friendship but his knowledge and wisdom – useful assets which I'd come to take for granted. But then, as Sam Friend said, 'You'll never miss the water till the well runs dry.' Knowledge and wisdom are perishable. It is a good thing that he condensed so much of his own, and others', into his books, and gave them such lucid and durable form.

DAVID GENTLEMAN

PREAMBLE

A revolution in the countryside

Since the beginning of this century there has been a revolution in the countryside, due chiefly to the new farming methods and the development of the motor-engine both as a means of power on the farm and as a link between the towns and the villages. But this revolution is not confined to a region or country or even to a continent: it is world-wide, and has occurred over precisely the same period – the first sixty or so years of this century. The First World War was the watershed in Britain. The old society, quickly changing even before 1914, emerged radically transformed after the Peace: the former rigid social caste system had been loosened; women had proved their ability to enter into industry, commerce, and the professions on equal footing to men; and the Corn Production Act of 1917 had at least recognized the need for defining a system of fair relations between the farmers and workers in the rural areas. It was not simply that a mode of life had greatly changed but a whole culture that had preserved its continuity from earliest times had now received its quietus, and was swept aside in less than a couple of generations.

The old rural community

The last generation of people who came to maturity under the old culture were those who were born about 1885, and not much later than 1895. It is true that people born after this date remember well the old pre-war society; but there is an important difference between these and the preceding generation: they lived their early years in this old society but they were too young to be formed by it. Their adolescence coincided with the Great War; and in many ways they were the first generation of the new age, the generation that escaped taking active part in the War but whose outlook it largely fashioned. The difference between these two generations is nowhere more sharply defined than in their attitudes to the traditional lore which is my main subject. The older generation had the lore in abundance; it was part of their existence and they had rarely paused to consider it as something separate from themselves. To a large extent it was not a question of believing in it but of living it. The next generation held a much attenuated version of the old culture and its lore. During the last fifteen years* I have talked to hundreds of people of both generations about the old society, and I have found this difference emphasized over and over again. The older generation accepted the old lore as part of the air they breathed; the later generation had already grown away from it. They knew much of the lore but they were sceptical, evaluative, and sometimes plainly dismissive.

The pattern under the plough

[My] subject bears an analogy to the crop marks seen in the aerial photographs of some of our fields. Just as the pattern of the ancient settlements is still to be seen in spite of years of repeated ploughings, so the beliefs and customs linked with the old rural way of life in Britain have survived the pressures and changes of many centuries. They are so old that they cannot be dated; and on this count alone they are historical evidence, as valuable as the archaeological remains that are dug from those sites so dramatically revealed since the development of the aeroplane.

*Written in 1965 [Ed.].

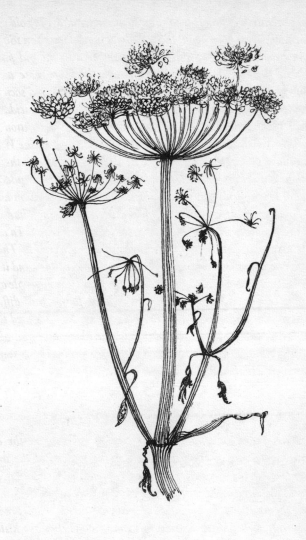

BLAXHALL

A Suffolk village

Blaxhall is a village of about four hundred people, six miles away from the Suffolk coast; and the east wind often blows the smell of the sea over the heathland. The cottages are tucked away in isolated groups between the fields. They are small brick-and-tile, box-like buildings, functional rather than picturesque. Their usual pattern is two rooms down and two upstairs; but there are a few *bedroom cottages* (bungalows) built originally by squatters on the common.

Most of the old people mentioned are natives of Blaxhall, but not one of them has lived continuously in the same cottage all his life: a change of master or retirement meant usually a change of house. Many of the cottages are still *tied* today [1956], so there is often a certain amount of moving about, but nearly always within the village. The cottages are so much alike that the moves do not seem to break the continuity of the various households: each family has its own nest of particular possessions – a pair of china dogs, a few old photographs, a couple of old chairs and a few pieces of old-fashioned china and a nineteenth-century clock; and these fit without any difficulty into the new home.

There is a sense of community existing among the old people, and they are secretly proud of belonging to Blaxhall. New-comers, hardy enough to attempt to settle in the village, are at first regarded from a distance and their behaviour is minutely observed just long enough to confirm the old judgement: 'Only the rum 'uns come to Blaxhall.'

A Blaxhall retrospect

The old pre-machine village community in Blaxhall was a tightly knit group, integrated for the carrying out of a particular work – the farming of the land and the many subsidiary trades and crafts directly connected with that farming. Mutual dependence, close ties among neighbours, was not merely a virtue: it was a necessity. Owing to the nature of the old hand-tool economy, farming could not be carried on except by the aid of a large group of people. At harvest-time, for example, there were crowds of reapers in the field, crowds also of women and children tying up the sheafs of corn and doing other light but necessary jobs. The whole village concentrated its efforts to see that the harvest went smoothly. Everybody was involved; and if something went wrong – a broken trace, a cracked felloe on a wagon-wheel or a horse dropping a shoe – someone in the village was ready to put it right; and the ritual of the harvest made it a truly communal occasion. Today, the harvest in the most highly mechanized districts is merely the chief incident in the rural year. Where twenty men formerly spent three weeks with scythes or binders harvesting the corn, today a couple of men with a combine-harvester will do the same work in a few afternoons; and if something goes wrong while they are at their work, the farmer

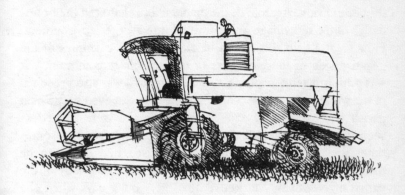

will probably have to send to the nearest town, perhaps even further, to get the spare parts for his combine. Full mechanization, that is, has had two main effects: it has gradually made most of the labour and many of the old village trades redundant; but – just as important – it has thrown back the virtual boundaries of the village so that it would be very difficult to say where exactly those boundaries lie today.

Any attempt to 'fix' a village in the past, to preserve the old ways and customs artificially, is misguided romanticism, wrong in its conception and impossible of application. It cannot be stated too emphatically that there is nothing to be gained by bemoaning the passing of the old community. The village has never stood still; its form has never been constant; and although the speed of recent change is making village life today both uncomfortable and disturbing, it does offer in addition an interesting challenge to those who are convinced that the small rural village has a future and who are actively concerned with helping it to evolve a new form.

But we can point to two great advantages which the machine has already brought to the countryside. It has largely taken the back-breaking and debasing toil out of farming – a tremendous gain in itself; and it has given to the farm-worker the conditions for better living. Again, . . . the machine has shattered the boundaries of the old village and admitted it to a larger environment. How great a gain this is can be shown by two examples of the negative side of the closeness of the old village community. It was self-sufficient, a compact rural unit; but it was also parochial in the worst sense of the word. The people who lived in the next parish were strangers, even 'foreigners'; and were treated as such in all dealings with them. Ordinary commerce was sometimes inevitable, but any intimacy was frowned upon: to be married to one of them was almost a crime. An old lady in the parish of Needham Market recalled her young days when she was rash enough to walk out with a man from the next parish. Her father's command, although ultimately ineffective, was direct enough: 'You must not do it! I can't have a daughter o' mine a-courting one o' those owd Creeting *jackdaws.*' Creeting is a village less than half a mile away, at the other side of the river.

A SHEPHERD'S LIFE

Back'us boy and shepherd

Robert Lionel Savage, the last of a long line of shepherds, died in his seventy-seventh year. But he 'gave up the sheep' some time before, badly crippled by the rheumatism that attacks so many of his calling. After years of rigorous lambing seasons when he was exposed to all kinds of weather and when the needs of the sheep were preferred to his own, he was anchored to his chair; and his mind easily swung back to the time when he started his career.

He left school at the age of twelve after satisfying the local schools inspector that he had reached a sufficient standard of learning to seek a job. He then went as *back'us* (back-house or kitchen) boy to a big farm in the village. The back'us boy was at that time the lowest rank in the rural hierarchy. He was under the command of the farmer's wife. She called and the back'us boy answered; and the calls he answered were many and various. A list of Robert Savage's duties gives an idea of the back'us boy's working day.

He rose at six-thirty in the morning and his first job was to give the milking pails to the cowman. These were kept indoors for the sake of cleanliness and the cowman would have to come

to the kitchen door to fetch them. He next made the copper-fire so that there would be plenty of water for the maids to carry upstairs for the family to wash. After the copper came the *blackstocks* – the open, barred fire-grates which would be lighted either for warmth or for cooking. Then as he turned from the blackstocks he would see numerous pairs of boots and shoes which the maids had set out in the back-kitchen waiting to be cleaned. These were the footwear of the farmer's family and of the guests who happened to be staying in the house; and had to be taken upstairs by the maids before 'they' rose. His next job was to grind coffee for the cook; and he was also under her eye as he did his next job which was cleaning all the knives. The knives were made of steel and they were cleaned daily with bath-brick and a board specially kept for the purpose. He would just have time to feed the fowls before breakfast time at nine o'clock.

The fare for breakfast was usually herrings and salt pork. 'They were wunnerful people for herrings.' The herrings were smoked or bloatered and enough were bought to last a week:

they were strung up on a line across the back-kitchen. Robert Savage was not happy with the breakfast when he first went to the farm because, as he said, 'Warm herrings and cold fat pork didn't fare to go right togither.' The girls used to go for the pork as they also went for the oatmeal porridge: the back'us boy, however, preferred the hominy – coarsely ground maize, boiled with water – that was an alternative to the porridge.

After breakfast came prayers. The girls filed into the drawing-room first and knelt down at the front. The back'us boy with the groom and any other male members of the household knelt behind them. Robert Savage confessed to tickling the girls in front of him to make them laugh: he was bored during prayers and would loiter over his breakfast purposely to get out of attending them. But after one of the family had read and a hymn had been sung, the servants would be released to their various tasks. The back'us boy's duties now took him outside: first to get the vegetables for dinner – potatoes, cabbages, roots, *sparrow-grass* (asparagus), anything that was in season. Then he chopped the kindling wood and filled the old brass-bound coal-scuttles and carried them into the house; next he peeled the potatoes for the cook.

Dinner was eaten about one-thirty, after the family had eaten theirs. The fare in the kitchen was the food that was left over from the dining-room. In the afternoon the back'us boy fed the fowls again, fetched the cows from the marshes; collected the eggs and did all kinds of jobs about the kitchen – any job that would turn up. Then came tea; and as soon as tea was cleared away and one or two little odd jobs completed, the last task was to take the letters up to the post office, about three-quarters of a mile away. This had to be done before six-thirty. If there were no evening jobs he could stay up in the village; this gave him a chance to visit his home and play with his friends. Whatever he did he had to be back at the farm before nine o'clock. But on some evenings he had to go back to dig in the garden; or if there were visitors he had to stand by to help with their horses when they went home. This was a better job than digging in the garden as the visitors invariably gave him a tip. There were other occasional and seasonal jobs such as churning the butter. This was done once a week during the winter; twice a week during the summer.

Wages were £1 a quarter, but there were some perquisites. He received a penny a score for the eggs he picked up about the farm. If one of the farm-workers discovered a hen's nest in a hedge or in the stack-yard, he would mark it by putting up a stick near it so that the back'us boy could find the nest and get his penny, or at least part of it. There would be occasions when the back'us boy was able to repay this kindness: for instance, when he was told to go down the cellar and draw beer for the gardener or the groom or any one of the workers who were entitled to a daily fixed amount, he would not be over-scrupulous about passing the fixed mark in the beer can.

The back'us boy also received a penny for plucking each fowl that was sold from the farm. The plucking of fowls that were consumed in the household was considered as part of his duty and there was no extra payment for these. For *drawing* – removing the entrails – and plucking a fowl to be sold he received twopence. All the little sums accruing to the back'us boy would be entered in the egg-book. The farmer's wife kept this in the knife-drawer in the kitchen, and often Robert Savage used to examine the book surreptitiously to see how much money he was accumulating.

'Sometimes I used to stop up to see to Old George's – the master's – horse if he was out late. Ephraim Row, the groom, would say to me sometimes that he didn't fare to be well and he'd ask me to see to the horse when the master came back. Old George used to go out in a *sulky* – a light kind o' trap; you was all boxed up in it and you couldn't fall out. So I would set up in the kitchen a-talking to the gels: sometimes it would be nigh midnight before the master came back; but they niver said nawthen to me when I was gettin' up for him. I remember Old George didn't come back one night till close on midnight. I saw to his horse; fed him and wiped him down; and then I went to the back'us door to go in. But I found it was locked. Young George had gone out to feed his dawg afore going to bed and he'd locked the back'us door thinking that Ephraim Row had seen to his father's horse and had gone home – he used to sleep at his own house did Ephraim – so I was locked out. I was thirteen or fourteen at the time and I didn't want to go round to the front door: there was nothing for it but to go home. So I went off up the road and I knocked up my father with the linen-prop and I told him: "I hevn't got a bed to sleep in." And he came down tidy quick and opened the door, and I turned in that night with brother Will. I didn't go down to the Grove till nine o'clock next morning. There was something to do down there, I can tell you: no hot water to wash nor nawthen! There was a kind o' official meetin' after I got down there to find out what it was all about. But it couldn't be helped and it all passed over.'

After he had been a back-house boy for about two years Robert Savage went to help with the horses. He also assisted the shepherd at various times, especially during the lambing season. Shepherding was, in fact, his true interest; and when he was sixteen he 'drew off' – he ceased to live in the farmhouse – and went to tend the sheep; and he spent the rest of his working life with them. Sheep-tending was in his blood; therefore when the

shepherd fell sick and the farmer offered to put him in sole charge of the flock with a man's wage he could not resist.

He went straight from being shepherd's *page*, as he termed himself, to take the full responsibility of the flock. This must have caused him a certain amount of hesitation at the time: 'I was so young,' he said, 'that I dursn't stay out in the dark by myself. I was not man enough to stay with the flock throughout the night; so for a little while my father used to come out with me at night and sleep in the little ol' cabin along o' me. But I soon got used to it by myself and I took no notice of the queer little noises you hear in the night. I kept with the shepherding at the Grove until they gave up the sheep altogether; then I moved to a farm in the next parish.'

'Us shepherd chaps had to be serious chaps. The farmers would let us git on by ourselves. You were independent and you had to think forrard. You can't say with sheep: "I'll do this now and maybe I'll do that tomorrow." You got to wait and do everything in its turn. You got to think forrard. And you can't break into something different when you a-shepherding. I couldn't give my hid (head) to anything else until after I'd given up the sheep. Though you got plenty of time when you are with the sheep, 'cos shepherding is a lonely life. You got no one to talk to. For the whole fore part of the day, when you took them up to the walks you wouldn't see a soul.'

The shepherd would have to wait until the lambing sales before he got his lambing-money; but some years he was compelled to ask for it before in order that he could buy shoes for his growing family. As well as the actual wages there were two or three perquisites. First the shepherd got a half a coomb of malt (two bushels) during lambing times in the same way as the other farm-workers got a similar amount during harvest. Also, every time he killed a sheep he was entitled to the *hid and pluck*. The head was cleaned and the *pluck* – the liver etc. – was boiled with it in the same pot to 'make a wunnerful stew for poor people'.

Robert Savage's sheep-dogs

The dog has always been the shepherd's essential helper. Robert Savage had many different types of sheep-dog during his shepherding days. One of the best was a bob-tailed dog – an Old English sheep-dog. He was a 'rare good dog'; very quick and intelligent and as gentle as a maid. But he had one fault; he was lazy in the summer. This, however, was not due to any inherent bad nature; his drowsiness was caused by the thickness of his coat. For in the heat of a summer's day he would have to slink panting into the shade; and there he would lie down at odds with the weather and with himself; and there he would stay irresponsive to his master's call. Yet if there was a pond or a full ditch into which he could plunge he came out refreshed and worked the sheep with vigour.

Many *crosses* with the Old English sheep-dog were tried: the cross with a terrier was of no use because the dog would *hang* – bite the wool and often actually nip the skin of the sheep; the cross with the wolf-dog (Alsatian) was more successful:

'Some people didn't trust the wolf-dogs, but they were wholly fine dogs and bred for sheep over in France; and the cross would make a fine sheep-dog. The red collies were stately, good-looking dogs, but they were not as useful as the crosses. The best dog iver I had was the first cross of an Old English sheepdog with a red collie. She wor called Nellie – a bitch she

[15]

wor. She would do something that no other dog I had iver did; and the rum thing was, no one iver larned her to do it (it must have been in the breed) as soon as iver I'd make for the gate – I didn't want to lift a finger or say nawthen – she'd up and round the sheep in a twinkle. And she'd soon have them following arter me: she kept behind them and had them as close together as folk at a wedding. I remember one morning I was working her and she suddenly walked off and wouldn't come back when I called. I was whoolly roiled. Then I went up to the hut and found she got underneath, made a kind o' hollow and had pupped. I took her and the family home; but I had to keep working her because I had no other dog for sheep. So I used to take her and her pups to the sheep in a donkey cart; and during the day the family would be underneath the cart and she'd lay with them whenever she got a chance.'

Bread-making

Priscilla Savage – or Prissy, as she is known – Robert Savage's wife, has had a life typical of that of a woman married to a farm-worker who had to bring up a large family on low wages. She sometimes complained with a humorous resentment about her husband: 'He knew little of it, because he was always looking after his precious sheep: most of my babies were born in the spring, and, of course, he was a-seeing to his precious lambs!' After she left school Priscilla Savage went as kitchen girl to one of the big farms in this parish. Later she 'went away foreign' – to service in a doctor's house in Essex; but after a few years there she returned and got married. She and Robert Savage first set up house on twelve shillings a week.

With so little money few things could be bought in the shops and people rarely went out to buy things in the town; the village was almost entirely self-supporting, most families living on what they grew or reared on their *yards* or allotments. There was no butcher, no baker or public bakery, and most households brewed their own beer. The Three B's – Bread, Bacon and Beer – were the staple articles of diet.

Bread was made at home from flour ground at the village mill; and the wheat in many families had been grown on the *common yard*, or had been given by the farmer as part of the harvest allowance. Many of the old brick ovens in which the bread was baked are still in existence in this village, but none of them is used now. In most cottages the brick oven is in the kitchen; but

behind a group of cottages in one part of the village there is a small outhouse containing a large brick oven, a *two-pail* copper and a *six-pail* copper, used for baking, the cooking of pig-products, and brewing respectively. This outhouse was at one time undoubtedly used by more than one of the cottages. The brick oven is beautifully constructed of a domed arch of bricks; and the skill of the old bricklayers must have been considerable, so perfectly do the bricks form the pattern of the arch, and so well has it survived its numerous firings.

Prissy's family of ten had two bakes a week, using altogether five stones of flour. The flour was often mixed with the whey left after making butter or cream cheese at the farm. The yeast was saved from the last brewing of beer; it was called *barm* and was kept in a cool earthenware jar on the floor of the larder. It would keep up to six months without going sour. But before Prissy mixed the dough she had to make sure she had plenty of fuel to heat her oven. This had to be heated by burning the fuel inside it. Apart from the door there is no outlet in a brick oven: the chimney is at the front just outside the oven door and when the fuel is burning the oven door is left open and the smoke escapes through that. The fuel used was most commonly *whin* faggots – the *bones* of *sere* or dry gorse – bound with elm withes. The process of making them was described by Prissy: 'You tied the whin faggots with green ellum withes. You put your foot on the bottom of a withe then you could rave the top of it like an S.' Broom was sometimes used for fuel: so also was heather. The heather was first stacked and pressed into bundles: it was preferred by some folk because, they said, it gave more heat. The fuel was thrust into the oven with a long-handled fork kept specially for the purpose. This fork was also used to stir up the embers until they burned completely out, leaving no smoke at all. It took about an hour for a brick oven to become properly heated for the dough. The bricks would change in colour from black to red as they got hotter; and when a handful of flour, thrown lightly against the side of the oven, burned up with a blaze of sparks, the housewife knew that her oven was hot enough for baking.

But before the dough went in the oven the ash would be scraped out and stowed in a hole beneath the oven. This was done with an ordinary garden hoe or with the *peel*, a long-handled spade-like tool used to slide in the tins of dough. While the oven was being heated the dough would have been rising in an earthenware pan covered with a cloth and placed near the oven. Just before the oven was ready the dough was placed into tins or kneaded into the shape of cottage loaves which were baked on the actual floor of the oven.

The actual placing of the dough into the oven was called *a-settin' in*. It was a job that had to be done quickly and smoothly so that the oven door was open for as little time as possible. When the housewife was *a-settin' in* everything else had to wait; even the doctor calling to examine one of the children would have to see the oven door closed before he could get her attention.

The bread would be done in about an hour. Often, however, the housewife took advantage of the heated oven to bake other things, risking the fact that by opening the door the bread might go *dumpy* or flat. One housewife in this village cooked her weekly joint of meat in the same oven as the bread. The meat, which took about two hours to cook, was placed at the back of the oven; then came the bread; and in front of the bread, at the edge of the oven, she placed two or three tins of Suffolk rusks which were done in about ten minutes and could quickly be withdrawn.

Small pieces of charcoal – the embers left from the fuel – often adhered to the loaves of bread that had not been baked in tins. These bits of charcoal gave an extra flavour to the bread according to the old people who are generally very critical of modern shop bread. They say that no bread has the flavour of the home-baked bread. It was made from stone-ground flour with all the goodness of the wheat grains left in it; and, therefore, it was much more sustaining than the present-day bread. It needed to be, for a meal in these days would often consist – apart from a hunk of cheese – almost entirely of bread, and before the coming of breakfast cereals many country children started their day with a 'mess of bread and hot skimmed milk'.

Stone-picking

Robert and Priscilla Savage, as parents of a large family, had great experience of stone-picking, and they have related how the practice was carried on. Stones were taken off the fields when the corn was about two inches high. The men raked some of the land overnight in order to loosen the stones so that the women and children could pick them the more easily the next day. The tool they used for this was the *daisy-rake* which was designed in the first place for raking clover. It was a wooden rake with six-inch nails, closely set together, serving as *tines* or prongs. The farmer would allocate a field to one family, and Robert Savage remembered Church Walk, a field near the church, best of all. 'It was a whoolly good field for stoon-picking. It wor like a shingle-beach: you could hear the old plough a-grinding through the stoons as it turned it over!'

Each picker took an ordinary two-gallon pail which could hold about a peck of stones. The pails were filled and the stones were dumped in a heap in the furrow: each heap had to be twenty bushels, or a *load*; and since there are four pecks in a bushel eighty pails of stones were required to make a load. To calculate how many pails the family carried the mother dug a small hole near the heap, and into this hole she would drop a small pebble for each pail of stones added. These were the *tally stones*, and Prissy recalls: 'If you weren't some careful the mischieful boys would keep a-dropping stoons into the hole on the sly so that they get done the sooner; but it wor no use, the farmer would know when he came to measure up the load if there wor some pails missing from it.' The boys often had to pick two or three buckets of stones before going to school in the morning.

Robert Savage has provided a coda to the old practice: 'You had to pick stoons at that time o'day if you wanted to keep the children tidy. Some of the children today don't know they're alive – they don't pick stoons or nawthen. But they stopped taking the stoons a good few years back. They could git them cheaper from up the *Sheres* (shires) somewhere. They used to come up the river in barges – grut big ol' stoons as big as this lil' ol' burd-cage.'

CHILDHOOD

Child labour

'If you lived in the country as I do, you would sometimes see a sight which would make your blood run cold, and yet it is so common a sight that we country people grow accustomed to it. You would see a great lumbering tumbril, weighing a ton or two with two wheels nearly six feet high, loaded with manure, drawn by a great Suffolk cart-horse as big as an elephant; and conducted by a tiny thing of a boy who can hardly reach the horse's nose to take hold of the rein; and, even if he can, has neither the strength nor weight to make such a huge monster feel, much less obey. Some of these urchins are employed upon the highroad which is comparatively safe for them. It is when they come into the fields with deep wheel-tracks, as deep nearly as half their little legs, it is turning into gate spaces where the children are obliged to cling to the horse's bridle and stumble along tip-toes, that the danger is.'

LATE 19TH CENTURY

The farmers wanted cheap labour and the parents wanted money; and these two facts conspired to keep many children out of school when they should have been at their desks. In fact many of them must have spent as much time working on the land as they did at school. The third entry in the school log-book reads: 'Numbers low. Boys wanted for field work.' A few weeks later a number of children were away picking up potatoes; and at the end of October they were again absent gathering acorns as winter-fodder for pigs. About this time, too, but in the following year a number of children were absent harvesting beet – cattle beet or mangle-wurzels. In November the head teacher wrote: 'Forty-five boys given permission to go out *brushing*.' The boys were away acting as brushers at a partridge shoot, beating the undergrowth with sticks to rouse the birds and drive them on to the guns. And so it went on all through the year. In January the teacher was worried because boys and girls were absent picking up stones and flint chips from the fields. They were paid for doing this by the farmers who carted away the stones, as already mentioned, to use as metalling for the roads.

In February and March they were often out of school employed in crow-keeping, bird-keeping or tending as the entries put it. That meant they were out scaring birds – rooks, crows, magpies and pigeons – keeping them away from the fields that had just been sown with spring corn. In many years they were out doing this again in the month of June, when the corn was just beginning to ripen. The children would be given a wooden rattle or clapper to scare the birds. Sometimes they made their own rattle by placing pebbles in a tin; sometimes they

just had to keep shouting. In some districts there was a traditional form of shouting to scare the birds; and there were many
rhymes or scaring songs which were sung in between the noise
made by a wooden clapper:

> *We've ploughed our land, we've sown our seed,*
> *We've made all neat and gay;*
> *So take a bit and leave a bit:*
> *Away, birds, away!*

Dibbling beans

The Helmingham schoolmaster, Henry Orchard, wrote on 20
February, 1874: 'Large numbers have been absent working on
the fields "dropping" beans and peas. Thin attendance in consequence.'

This proves that the farmers also employed children when
they dibbled beans and peas. But for beans, at least, some
farmers were already using the bean-drill. This was a kind of
hod attached to the plough. The beans dropped into the furrow
as it was turned over; and they were covered up by another
plough following behind and turning another furrow.

It was in such areas as Helmingham, where dibbles have been
used without interruption right up to the present, that some of
the lore connected with them has survived. Here are two rhymes
which the children recited occasionally while dibbling, to break
up the monotony of the work:

> *Four seeds in a hole:*
> *One for the rook, and one for the crow;*
> *And one to rot, and one to grow.*

or:

> *Four seeds in a hole:*
> *One for the buds (birds),*
> *One for the meece (mice),*
> *And two for Maaster.*

Crusts of bread and buck-soup

The living conditions of the school children varied from village to village. William Spalding, a stallion leader, knew some of the worst:

'There were nine of us and we had a very hard time to get enough food to live. We had to work very hard after tea, after we come home from school, doing various jobs like carting wood and so on. I had no boots in them days. And I know what it was like to fling a crust of bread and dripp'n' away one day and go looking for it the next because I was so hungry. I was often hungry. And I used to pick the oats out of the bowl – what the horses had to eat from – plenty of times.'

At Helmingham during the lean times no children went as hungry as this. Mrs D. Manning recalls:

'During the worst part of the winter – that would be just before Christmas or just after – Lady Tollemache used to provide soup for the poorer families. We used to fetch the soup from the Hall when school finished. It was venison soup from the deer in the park. They used to kill so many deer a week and then boil up the venison in a big copper. *Buck-soup* we used to call it. The bigger boys and girls, if the mothers couldn't go, used to bring their cans to school and then they'd be let out at half past eleven to go up to the Hall and fetch it – which they could do and leave it until they went home from school. And sometimes the lids came off the cans and two sticks went in to fish out a piece of meat before we reached home.'

The boon makes the frame

Sam Friend of Framsden, Suffolk, has been a farm-worker all his life apart from his war service during the First World War; but he has become a kind of rural philosopher with an earthy wisdom and an apt word – usually a dialect one – for most aspects of the old culture. He points out the main difference between the conditions affecting the children of his 'young time' and the position today:

'Some of 'em didn't have enough to eat; though, of course, at that time o' day what you did have you had to *stay*. I mean they used to bake the bread in the oven and brewed – home-brewed beer; and some of the ones who were better off they'd have pork in the pot. But if there was a family of five or six children what could they have with wages as they were? Ten or twelve shillings a week!

'It's like this: those young 'uns years ago, *I said*, well – it's like digging a hole, *I said*, and putting in clay and then putting in a tater on top o' thet. Well, you won't expect much will you? But now with the young 'uns today, it's like digging a hole and putting some manure in afore you plant: you're bound to get some growth, ain't you? It will grow won't it? The plant will grow right well. What I say is the young 'uns today have breakfast afore they set off – a lot of 'em didn't use to have thet years ago, and they hev a hot dinner at school and when they come home most of 'em have a fair tea, don't they? *I said.* These young 'uns kinda got the frame. Well, that's it! If you live tidily that'll make the marrow and the marrow make the boon [bone] and the boon make the frame.'

Lambs'-tail pie

Mrs Tom Jay's father was shepherd to John Goddard of Tunstall, and she remembers going out to him into the field during lambing time, over seventy years ago:

'I used to go out to my father's hut early in the morning. He had a little stove in his hut – I think it's still here in the house – and he used to warm the milk for the lambs on this little stove. Then came the time when he used to cut off the lambs' tails – he used to burn 'em off with a hot iron. Then he'd skin the tails and bring 'em home. And Mother used to stew 'em a little; then she used to take 'em out of the saucepan, cut them up and make a lovely lambs'-tail pie with potatoes and so on. It was delicious. I can taste it now. Delicious. But they have some other way of doing lambs today: they don't burn their tails off as they used to.'

Sparrow stew and sparrow dumpling

Nothing I have collected about the social conditions which were the background to children's attendance at school reveals the true position better than the accounts of catching sparrows for the pot. For the food many of the children ate, as well as being insufficient, was greatly lacking in protein. Meat was too expensive to buy, and if a family had no pork in the pot there was likely to be a grave imbalance in the diet. Many families were able to correct this by the poaching of rabbits, game and hares. But there was also a widespread and more legitimate custom of catching sparrows. At Tunstall, Mrs Tom Jay recalls, there was a *Sparrow Club*; and members of the Club used to go round the stacks of a well-disposed farmer, John Goddard, netting the birds – usually at night:

'My brother used to bring them home and I'd skin them and open the breasts and stew them; and if we'd got a piece of pork it went into the stew with them. Sometimes I'd put the sparrows in a pie with different things to flavour it.'

Her husband, Tom Jay, added:

'Those were hard times, they were: get what you could get and eat what you could eat. There was no picking this and picking that like there is today. I used to work at Snape maltings. I worked there for over twenty year; and at the time of year when there was snow on the ground (we seemed to get more snow then than we do now) the sparrows would come into the maltings for food, picking up grain and so on. And I'd trap as many as forty and bring 'em home and skin 'em. We used to boil them up in a saucepan or a boiler: we'd make a soup out of them.'

Sam Friend has also caught sparrows:

'Yes, I've been round of a night after sparrows. We used to have a lot of fish-netting, and we'd arrange and leave it hanging at the front. Then we'd hev a bull's-eye lantern and we'd shine it on the net, and they'd go in and you'd see them bright and then you'd trap 'em. We used to flay 'em – take their clothes off – and cook 'em in a basin with a crust on top. We used to call it *sparrow dumpling*. A lot o' people never tasted meat, and that were better than no meat at all.'

Underclothes

Mrs Priscilla Savage told me how school children managed for clothes in an open village:

'My mother used to make us underclothes. They had a brown colour. What we called quilted stays which had three buttons down the front and, of course, button-holes: we had brown calico chemise and knickers made from the same stuff. They

were all made from the Garthwayte calico that was given to the parish of Blaxhall. Every year each family had a sheet and a yard of calico for each child. They gave it out in the church porch. There were two shopkeepers. Mr Mannall would see to half the village: Stone Common and up to Stone Farm and the Church Common; and Mr Gibson used to have Mill Common and the Ship Corner – this end of the village. They'd have two tables on each side of the church porch and they'd have their rolls of calico there and they'd cut it up and give it out. Arthur Gibson's calico was better than Mr Mannall's. It was tuppence ha'penny a yard, but still that was good calico. That was the underclothes made from calico. And you had red flannel or pink flannelette out of what your mother left off. For my own boys I used to make little wool jerseys and little cord trousers, and we used to knit a kind of fisherman's socks for them to go to school with.'

Boots

Boots were one of the most difficult problems; and the farm-worker of this period always tried to fit out the children with boots out of the money he got from harvest. But Mrs Savage gave me an example of how dearly a pair of boots was prized in a family; and, incidentally, how well made were the boots ordered from the village shoe-maker. She left school to go into domestic service:

'I went when I was eleven; and my father wasn't a strong man so, of course, my mother couldn't afford to buy things. She took the bottom of two of his shirts and the odd sleeves; and out of the best parts of the shirts she made me two print dresses. One was a blue and white plaid and the other was red and white which in them times was called the *Oxford shirting*. And she made me two print dresses to start with. And my poor old father said, well, he would get me a pair of boots – which of course were made by our village shoe-maker, Mr Newson. He made me a pair of high kid-topped button boots. They were buttoned half-way up the calf of my leg, and I wore them for years and years. And I didn't dispose of them not till two years ago. And they were in there in the cupboard and I said to one of the boys: "I'm tired of seeing those old boots about," I said, "I'll dispose of them." But the buttons! I've really got some of the buttons now. You know the buttons. There were no end of buttons on them!'

Common lands

Charles Hancy, who was one of the users of Outney Common, Bungay, describes its use by a number of small-holders who were essentially 'country' townsmen, exactly like their medieval forebears, who had little land-use other than that provided by the common. Outney Common once ran right up to the north-west ditch of the town – part of the early defence works of the town against raiders coming up the River Waveney from the sea; and access to the common has little altered since the town's original siting. Except that Charles Hancy was formally regis-tered as a pupil at one of the town's state schools (although attending only infrequently because he was often comman-deered to help during school hours in his father's hay business), his daily routine was little different from that of a boy who lived in the town centuries before – going out of the town gate early each morning, either milking his cows or driving them on to the common; and milking them again or driving them home in the evening. From his description we get a true sense of what a late medieval town must have been like to live in:

'There were ten cow-keepers round here in Broad Street, Bungay. Down in Nethergate Street there, where I lived then, there were half a dozen cow-keepers down there, yes. My father had several cows. We used to have – every six o'clock in the morning – to go on the common to get the cows up. That's when they unlocked the gates. You couldn't get them up before six. The old bailiff used to come down there and unlock the gate. Nine times out of ten, you'd got all the cows up near the gate then. He'd just come and unlock 'em and let 'em off. We used to have to bring 'em, come home with them, shove a tin of corn in the manger for 'em, tie them up and set a-milking on 'em. Me and my sisters, we used to milk eight cows before we went to school. (I had two sisters: when they were at home they used to milk and all.) After we'd finished milking we'd go indoors, have a wash; and we used to take a can of milk up the street. My mother

[31]

used to come round with the milk: she'd take two big cans round the town; measure it out at your door; pint measure and half-pint measure. Milk was only a penny a pint then: some of them just had half a pint for a ha'penny. She used to take two cans; she carried these herself; and I used to take a big can up the street and leave it against the public house, the Swan, there, so that you didn't have to come home after more to finish the round. And I turned the cows out again. I had to sweep up all the droppings in the yard 'fore I went to school. And I used to have half a dozen cans of milk; I'd hawk them right down there to Bungay Common – take them to customers; and I'd go off to school, take the cans with you and bring them home at dinner-time.

'When you got home at dinner-time there was a full-time job again. There was – we used to mix up all the food. We had to grind – clean the beet first – grind them, mix up with the chaff. They used to be mixed up then. We then fed 'em with a bushel-skep; shoved the bushel of food in the manger for each cow, and then off you go to school again. Then when four o'clock time came just the same routine: home you come, straight down to the common-gate and get your cows off; and turn round and milk them; and arter you finished milking turned 'em out. And then you had to start cutting chaff for next day – cutting chaff and mixing up. All done by hand; the old beet-grinder and all: it used to shred it, you know, the old beet-

grinder. You used to shove the beet on top, fill the old machine up and then turn the handle; and then it'd come out. You'd stand the bushel-skep underneath, you see. (These old machines were made so you could shove a bushel-skep underneath them.) Fill it up, heap your chaff, level that off; and you'd chuck your beet on the top on it and mix it with a fork. That's how we had to do it then.

'I had two sisters, as I say, and they were brought up to the milking just the same. I was ten year old: the other boys wouldn't set along with me at school. I used to stink of owd cows, so they reckoned. I used to get into rare trouble over that. Yeh, ten year old. I had to do that!'

Pigs' pudding

'There was a market-day in Saxmundham and sale-day every other Wednesday, same as there is today. My father always had a pig or two in the sty; and we used to live on fat pork – pork and onion dumpling. They used to put 'em in a cloth; tie 'em up and put it in a saucepan and boil 'em up. And every Christmas – he allus had a pig or two in the sty – he'd go and give them a piece o' plum pudding. He say:

'"We'd better give the owd pigs a bit. We'll kill 'em in a fortnight's time!"'

HARRY CABLE

Annie Cable remembers

After Harry Cable had told me his story, his wife, Annie Cable, who later* recounted her life in service, went on to discuss their 'young days'. Mrs Cable said:

'We used to have fun in those days. But I don't know whether – I think I'd still like to come to the old times. I do, really and truly. I think the world today is really an upheaval, isn't it? No one is satisfied. There ain't no poor today. Do you know, when I was a little girl going to school, when eggs were so cheap, we used to have half an egg each! Didn't we?' Her husband agreed:

'You know when bloaters were twelve a shilling, we didn't have a whole one. I used to toss up with my brother to see who'd have the head and who'd have the tail. That's the truth! There's more in the head, ain't there?'

'But we were more contented. Once a year in the wagons to our school outing! Today children don't value no toy, no nothing. Do they? At least I don't think so. And there isn't no poor! Because look! When we got home from school we had what is called our *Saturday Clothes*. All our school clothes we used to have to take off, and put on any old thing that had been patched. And then we had to go to school when it was snowing (because we had more snow and frost in those days) with my dad's old woollen socks over our boots. There wasn't such things as *water-boots* in them days. And another thing I used to do – I can remember it to this day – in the winter-time I used to get my boots; get the poker; get some hot ashes out of the grate; put 'em in the boots and shake 'em backwards and forwards like; and put them back again and put our feet in while our boots were warm.'

*See page 173.

RURAL LIFE

Village self-sufficiency

To imply that the old village formed an organic unit is not to sentimentalize it. The organism was in fact far from being healthy. There was intense poverty in it, especially during some periods, and there were the tensions that were inevitable where the old system of dependence on master or squire had retained its force long after it had lost its relevance and many of its benefits. But the conditions of farming in a largely self-sufficient community, where needs could be satisfied without moving out of the village, made for at least a formal unity in the rural group. Framsden mill and its environs will illustrate what I mean about the compactness and self-sufficiency of the rural villages in East Anglia. Stanley Ablett recalled the scene when the mill was in full production:

'Over there on the other side of the yard was the blacksmith's shop with the wheelwright and carpenter's shop next to it. In the cottage on the other side of the stables lived the village shoemaker. Then in Hill House, just outside the mill, where Mr Besley now lives, there was a grocer's shop kept by a Mr Flick who was also the village carrier, taking goods to and from Ipswich. In Hill House, too, a tailor used to work. That building

[35]

in the corner housed the old portable steam-engine that Mr Webster the miller later bought: he used to grind the corn there when there was no wind. Later still he got an oil engine; and people at that time could buy both coal and oil from the miller.'

Most of the village tradesmen were, therefore, within hailing distance of one another; and although this compactness undoubtedly made Framsden an exception, it was the condition that most villages tended to. Transport to the town was difficult and made for self-sufficiency and reliance on village resources. There was only one form of public transport, the carrier's horse and cart that went once or twice a week to the town, and even then with little room or encouragement for passengers. What remained for most villagers was: 'The Hobnail Express', as Sam Friend put it, 'Shanks's Pony: stay home or walk twelve miles to Ipswich and perhaps spend the night on Mother Greenfield's pillow on the way back.'

Black magic

'I wouldn't like to say that there is not such a thing as black magic but I know of a coincidence, or something that happened regularly. No one has been able to explain it to me (it's nothing to do with horses by the way). But it's a strange kind of thing that happened in this part of the country, the kind of story you get in Suffolk and Norfolk. There was this old girl at Blo Norton. Her son was the biggest poacher – he was a devil: he'd rob your house in the middle of the day and let you see him! But the police could never catch him. If they went to the house and saw him move into the door, they'd turn out the family, look everywhere and he was not to be found. But his mother would be sitting there with this black cat in her arms: she'd always got this black cat when he weren't there. The police would search the house and he was never there. And you never saw that cat when he was there! Now this will surprise you, I know; but my mother has pointed that out time after time. She said:

'"You go along that Blo Norton road and you'll never see the black cat unless Alby [we'll call him that, though that wasn't his proper name] if Alby had disappeared out of sight the black cat was there. You never saw the two together."

'People in the village said she was a witch. But this is . . . you can make of it what you like, can't you?'

MERVYN CATER

The Case is Altered

'Another story touching on wet days: poor old Mrs Suggett told me it. Narrowback was her husband. He was very short and very very broad-shouldered; and they called him Narrowback. She was a lovely old lady. When I was young she used to come up to my mother's for a cup o' tea; and I liked talking to the old lady. She lived in a house down the street at Brampton, a house that had been a pub; and the name of it was *The Case is Altered*. Well, she told me how it come to be closed.

'She said they would have what they called a *settin' in*. Well. I heard about that: when I was just twenty and used to go to these pubs – *The Dog* and so on – the boys there would talk about a settin' in. And a settin' in was what was happening at the pub – the reason it got closed. One or two of the boys would go in there, fellers of the village, and they would stop there all night, and the next night; and they say it had been known for it to go the week; have a week settin' in, staying in the pub. The landlord went and got 'em a snack if they liked one. They slept on the old settles, and they wouldn't go home. They'd leave 'em there. (In fact, owd Elshie Peck, here at *The Dog* – so the landlord used to tell me, owd Fred Quickmore – "He came on my valuation". He went over on the valuation when the pub changed hands – that was in my time – as part of the stock!) But getting back to *The Case is Altered*: I supposed that if the people got browned off, as

we call it, they'd have a settin' in. And on this particular occasion this feller (if you go along the Low Road and up Fishpond Lane, there's a farm up there: this feller came from that farm) and after a setting' in at *The Case is Altered* he died going up Fishpond Lane. And it was a terrible thing at that time o' day, if anybody died in the village. They all sort of mourned for him: to think that he died after a settin' in must have been terrible! Anyroad, I think Lord Stradbroke – he undoubtedly had a lot to do with keeping the people in order – he closed the pub. That must have happened somewhere about the middle of last century. The old lady, old Mrs Narrowback, she was a lady the biggest part of eighty in 1920, which takes you back to 1840. Yes, Lord Stradbroke went up there; and they thought the pub had become unruly, so they thought they'd better close it. That was *The Case is Altered.*'

HORACE WHITE

The cow in the tumbril

The scene is a farmyard where an empty, two-wheeled farm-cart or tumbril is standing under an open cart-shed, its shafts in the air: the chain, which when in use fits across the horse's wooden *pad* or saddle, is hanging loose between the shafts. The teller is Jack Page who lived at All Saints, Halesworth in Suffolk:

'I see a cow in a tumbril, dragging a tumbril! She got into it herself she did. And that was when I bin to Bungay with that there wagon. I believe I had the same two horses in that wagon;

and I was coming up the Bungay road past Mr Charlie Skinner's, and the yardman let them cows out to water, d'ye see, like they allus do every morning after they had milking done. And, of course, they – the tumbril was standing in the cart-shed there with the back-chains hanging, d'ye see, fixed on each shaft, just like they do when they go on a horse. I suppose one of them old cows – well, they stood there rubbing of their old rumps about like that, you know; and all at once this here tumbril fell down, and the back chain went right just over the front of har shoulders. Well, she come out of that there shed: well, you would have laughed if you'd ha' seen har. (And the chap is alive now, I expect, that lived down there in St Margaret's Low Street; and he come and stood like that there: he didn't know what to do. He couldn't do nothing about it!) Well, she went round that there yard two or three times there with the tumbril on one wheel; and then the other owd cows, they were going about there, you know. With their pump-handles up. Well there! You talk about going and – all I was afraid she was going to do – she was coming on to the road so she would run into me! Do [if she did], she'd ha' made a mess of me! 'Stead of that, she went round the corner of the stable, and she hit the corner of the barn and turned the tumbril right over, that did! And that laid there bottoms up when Mr Collyer come up with his throshing tackle at night, and he say:

'"Hullo!" he say, "what – you have a horse run away here?"

'And they told him this here cow run away. Of course it was right: this poor owd cow, she ran right across these fields there, what they call Brookey's Wood; and they had to go and fetch

her. Dear, oh dear! Heart alive! You talk about – didn't I laugh! I never forget it till the day I die. I shan't. No!

'I had two horses in the wagon that day: I had two that day. And I was alone. Well, there! I've never seen anything like it. I've told a lot of people about that, and they laughed fit to kill themselves. But that's the truth! She stood in there with her back-part against the tumbril; and it hadn't got a prop on it to keep it up, you see; of course she kept rubbing about, and 'course, down that come! And the chain come down on the top of har shoulders, and her neck – you see, the owd sore part of her neck, that cut in there. It must have hurt har because she was *a-bloring** good tidily; bloring out. Well, I tell you, she come out of the yard, and went round that level bit of ground agin that pond, on one wheel. Dear! Oh dear! Heart alive! I've seen a lot o' different things and that like; but I've never seen an owd cow dragging a tumbril!'

The Whitsun fair

In Blaxhall at Whitsun, a fair was regularly held in the village inn. Blaxhall Ship Inn Fair took place on Whitsun Wednesday.

*bellowing – *OED*: 1440, variant of *blare*.

A club existed with its centre at the inn and the landlord was the treasurer. Members of the club saved up during the year to celebrate the Fair. (An annual outing to the seaside has long ago displaced this occasion.) Some of the money saved went in prizes for the various competitions held during the day. One of the most popular of these competitions was *Sneering through a Horse-collar. Sneering* is the dialect for making an ugly face; and the best – or the worst? – *sneerer* took the prize. There was at one time a kind of folk-tale relating to this game in Suffolk. A curious old lady, seeing the horse collar hanging up in an unusual position, exclaimed peevishly: 'What's this for? What are they a-dewin' with this here?' She poked her head through the collar and was immediately awarded the prize.

Although none of the other Blaxhall competitions is connected with horse-gear, they are included as examples of the way farm-workers and their wives enjoyed a *frolic. Races* were a prominent part of the fair. These were held on the road outside the inn and the distances were: one mile, a half and a quarter of a mile. Trees along the road – some of the old people still remembered which particular trees – marked the starting points; and all the races finished at the inn. The prizes were packets of tea, sweets and beer – as men, women and children competed. At one point of the fair it was the tradition for the landlord to go upstairs with a frying pan full of *Hot Ha'pennies*. He scattered these from a window on to a sandy area just in front of the inn door. The antics of the children as they scrambled and tried to pick up the coins were one of the highlights of the day. *Drinking the Hottest Cup of Tea* was a competition reserved for the women. All the leather-tongued gossips competed; but one woman was invariably the winner. She had a *fake* – a trick: just before the contest started she smeared her mouth well with butter. While the women were competing the men were *Bowling for Nine-pins* at the back of the inn. Then in the evening the fun continued inside the inn: drinking and *Singing the Old Songs* to the tune of the 'cordion'. Folk-songs – many of them connected with the sea – were the chief items. There was also *Stepping* or *Dancing.* *Stepping* has always been a feature of this particular village and it is still practised to a certain extent today. In the old days the boys learned to *step* on two bricks. A great deal of the stepping seems to have been improvised but it also contained the remnants of old dances. One of these was the *Candlestick Dance*:

'You first tucked up your skirts between your legs and you danced backwards and forwards, round and about and over a lighted candlestick. The tune was *Jack be Nimble, Jack be Quick* played over and over again on the "cordion". If you put out the candle you were finished. I learned this dance from my mother. It's a very old dance. The men wore high-heeled boots at that time o' day. They were lovely boots; and they danced to the "cordion" usually; but if there was anything special on they had a fiddler.'

Priscilla Savage of Blaxhall gave most of the above information and she commented:

'You had to make your own fun at that time. Nobody hardly went out of the village; and it was up to people to make their own enjoyment. Whitsun week was a jolly time. Blaxhall folk used to say: "I like Whitsun Monday (Framlingham Fete), I like Whitsun Tuesday (another local frolic); and o' course I like Whitsun Wednesday; but *damn* Whitsun Thursday!" '

Suffolk cunning

A dealer in agricultural machinery took a beet-cutter to demonstrate to a farmer. The farmer called one of his men and said: 'Here, George, you have a go at it. Tell me what you think on it.' An old worker, after giving the machine a jaundiced look, turned the handle and tried it with a few roots. Asked what he thought of it he said with conviction: 'It's some stiff, maaster. It whoolly sticks when you turn thet wheel: I fare to think it wants greasin'.' 'Send for Copping [the dealer]; he's just across the field a-looking at that harrow,' said the farmer. The verdict *It wants greasin'* was repeated to the dealer; but as he was a Suffolk man himself he summed up the situation in a moment. So as soon as the farmer's back was turned he slipped a shilling into the old boy's palm – six pints o' beer at that time o' day' – and said to him: 'Just yew have a go at it now, bo'.' On being asked the second time by the farmer how the machine worked, the old worker said: 'It be whoolly fine now, maaster. It dew go like a rick on fire.'

BEES

Mr. Thompson's bees

Bees and the family

The close link of the bees with the household or family of their owner is a feature of northern mythology; and the custom of 'telling the bees' was practised in many north European countries until recent years. It was a common practice among the old rural community in East Anglia, and here is a typical account of it taken from a man who was born at Stonham Aspal, Suffolk:

'If there was a death in the family our custom was to take a bit of crepe out to the bee-skeps after sunset and pin it on them. Then you gently tapped the skeps and told the bees who it was who had died. If you didn't do this, they reckoned the bees wouldn't stay, they'd leave the hives – or else they'd pine away and die.'

In the village of Debenham there was an old bee-keeper who regularly talked to his bees and claimed to be able to interpret their response by the pitch of their buzzing. It is certain that bees are very responsive to different tones of the human voice, and this is probably the reason for the country belief that bees are peace-loving beings and will not stay with a quarrelsome family. Similarly it is likely that it is the basis of the injunction that 'you must never swear in the hearing of your bees'. A Suffolk man said: 'My grandfather was a bit of a rough diamond, and he wasn't above letting a few words fly in front of us children when he felt like it. But he would never use bad language when he was near his bees. He'd always be on his best behaviour then!'

But to return to the old bee-keeper:

'James Collins treated the bees as members of the family. He was a retired thatcher and he used to come and *work the bees*, as he said, at the saddler's where I was apprentice. This was well before the First World War. I used to carry the box up for him when he was going to smoke the bees out, and I was able to observe him pretty closely. If there was a tempest about – if the air felt thundery in any way – he wouldn't go near the bees. And at any time before approaching the hives he'd stand back and listen, to find out how they were getting on. Then he'd look to see which way they were travelling, so that he wouldn't get into their line of flight. He'd watch them quietly; and he often told me how he had a good idea where they'd been taking their honey: if they came to their hives low, they'd most likely have

Beeskep

come off a field of clover. If they had been working on fruit trees they'd come in much higher. It wouldn't do to get in their line of flight: you'd be sure to get stung. The old man told me in this connection:

'"If the bees come near you don't start beating the air: leave 'em. Don't fight the bees; the bees will allus win."

'It's true. The bees will stop a horse. And I thought of what Jim Collins said when I heard what happened over at Stonham. Just by the maltings there was a man cutting clover with a cutter and two horses. Everything was going on well till the machine broke down. The worst part about it was that it stopped right in the line of flight of some bees who were working the field of clover. They attacked the driver and he straightway made a bolt for it, leaving the horses standing there. Both horses were stung unmercifully. One of them died soon afterwards; and the other one – I saw it myself – was so bad and its head so swollen up with the stings that it had to be supported in its stable by a kind of sling fixed to the roof.'

LEONARD ALDOUS

But the bees not only knew the voice of their owner but also his particular smell: one bee-keeper told the writer: 'Whenever I go to the barber's I've always to tell him: "Nothing on, thank you." If he were to put lotion on my hair, however nice it smelled, the bees wouldn't think much of it at all. I know from experience that if I approached their hives with scented lotion on my hair it would make them angry.' The bees in fact should be treated at all times, so is the belief, as if they were people; and people who were very ready to take offence if not treated properly. They must not be bought or sold or even taken or given as a present. A bee-keeper may give away a hive, and later the recipient will find a way of unobtrusively repaying the kindness either with an appropriate gift or with some worthwhile service.

WILLIAM COBBOLD

WORKING THE LAND

In the field

In many ways the part of a horseman's job calling for most of his skill was that concerned with working the land, and using a standard of craftsmanship set immeasurably high both by the tradition of his craft and by the immediate needs of cultivation; and a horseman served a long and disciplined apprenticeship before he could attain to the standard demanded. Briefly, this meant the ability to 'take his work and leave it': to start and finish the ploughing; that is, to pen and shut up a furrow and leave every *stetch*, or parcel of furrows, straight and level and without a wrinkle to mar the whole length of it.

In Suffolk it was customary until recent years to plough a field in stetches or lands of varying widths. Each stetch was limited on its two sides by *water-cuts* or deep furrows that made easy the escape of surface water from the soil; and in fact the main purpose of ploughing in stetches was – and still is, where stetches continue to be used – to ensure effective draining of the land. The lighter the soil the fewer water-furrows were needed and, therefore, the wider were the stetches. In the *strong-loam* belt of Suffolk – the heavy-land districts – however, very narrow stetches of two yards and upwards were necessary effectively to take off the surface water. As the ploughshare most commonly used in this county was one that turned a nine-inch furrow, the two-yard stetches were characterized as *eight-furrow work*; the two-and-a-half yard stetches as *ten-furrow work*; and the three-yard as *twelve-furrow*. But the narrow stetches were used only where the heaviness of the land made them inescapably necessary; for their disadvantages were many. First of all, the more water-furrows in a field the more land is wasted; secondly a field that is ploughed in narrow stetches that are ridged up slightly to assist the drainage is not the best seed-bed for a crop of corn, as the ridges are bound, to some degree, to cause an unequal ripening of the seed. Again, as it was impossible for wheeled implements to cross the frequent deep water-cuts of a field ploughed in this way, all cultivation had to be done along the stetch itself; and this meant that implements – drills, hoes, harrows, etc. – had to be adapted to fit the width of stetch used.

But the introduction of the reaping machine, the self-binder and latterly the combine-harvester made the use of narrow stetches impossible, as the continual jolting over the deep furrows soon put the most robust machine out of action. Under the surface draining or *thorough water-draining* of the land had to be undertaken on a more planned and workmanlike scale than had been done formerly; for now the below-surface drains had to take off *most* of the water and conduct it to the ditches, and had not merely to assist the wasteful system of frequent water-furrows on the surface, as the old bush-drains had done when they were almost the sole method of under-draining. Therefore

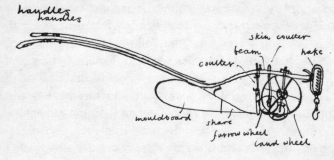

the narrow stetches gradually went out of use as more machinery was introduced, and they were replaced by *flat-work* – wide stetches with water-furrows at as great an interval as was compatible with efficient overall draining.

But when the first baiter* led his teams on to an unploughed field he did not have to trouble his head about the width of the stetches: that had been fixed by long usage and probably appeared to him then as unalterable an aspect of the landscape as the roads and the hedges. His first job was to start his teams to plough: he had already been on the field the day before to mark out the stetches. He had laid out their width, at each end of the field, with the help of a *stetch-pole*, a pole equal in length to the width of the stetch they were working – a nine-foot one in twelve-furrow work. This use of a pole to measure arable land is very ancient. Old Welsh laws, quoted by Seebohm, specify how the strips of plough-land were to be measured – in some provinces – with a rod equal in 'length to the *long-yoke* used in ploughing with four oxen abreast'.

At each end of the centre or *top* of the stetch he placed a hazel-stick, taken from the hedge and peeled so that the white pith acted as a *sight* for drawing his first furrow. He, or the second horseman, did this for the whole of the field until it was marked out in equally spaced stetches. He then drew the first furrow of the stetch himself. If the first furrow was straight, example and actual guidance helped to persuade the ploughman who followed after him to draw the other furrows in the stetch in like manner: if the first furrow was *bent* nothing could prevent the others from being less than perfect also. The responsibility for drawing the first furrow on a narrow stetch was one the head horseman could not afford to delegate, unless it was to a man equally skilled as himself; for a stetch that did not come out, at every point, exactly to the inch would render ineffective the use of implements that had been designed specially for it; again, a botched stetch was visible to all – to the casual passer-by and to

*The head horseman.

[49]

the practised eye of his neighbour; and the 'loss of face' a head horseman suffered through allowing the standard of his own work to be below that of the next farm's was enough to make him ensure that every field was laid out and ploughed with as much care as patience and long-practised skill made possible. But another important reason for the head horseman's care was that he was directly responsible to the farmer for the way the field was cultivated; and if the farmer brought forward a complaint, the head man had to bear the full burden of it.

After he had drawn the first furrow in the stetch he returned alongside, ploughing a second furrow against the first, thus completing the *laying of the top* or centre-furrows – in shape, exactly like the ridge of a roof. He then left the first stetch and did the same with the next.

Perhaps the deep concern of the horsemen to keep their high standard of work even in the ordinary day-to-day ploughing can best be understood when we look at it against the background of a practice that was once common in many parts of Suffolk. On

Sunday mornings during the time of the spring and autumn ploughing, the horsemen often strolled around the parish to view one another's work, estimating its quality with the eye for detail of an exacting *sticker** at a furrow-drawing match. And if a man had a *bent* furrow or a *hog's trough* (a hollow between two furrow slices) in his work, the mistake would soon be recorded in every farm and public house in the parish.

Arthur Chaplin's account

Arthur Chaplin has given an account of the responsibility of the first baiter in the field:

'Supposing he had to plough a field of thirteen acres and he had eight plough-teams working. His first job was to calculate when they should finish, how long they should take to plough the whole field, each man ploughing at the rate of three-quarters of an acre in one day. Next he had to calculate how many *rounds* each man had to plough. Then he had to remember that even after the rounds had been allocated and the stetches accounted for, he still had to include the acre or so of *headland*, the land on the outside of the field where the ploughs turned, which had to be ploughed the last of all.'

The procedure followed at Stowupland with the twelve-furrow work was similar to that already described for the ten-furrow: the head horseman, or first baiter, laid the top and the other horsemen followed him, each ploughing a round at least on a stetch.

'If there were only six stetches in the field and eight ploughs working, the first baiter then put the second baiter and another to open up the furrows and lay the tops, so all the ploughs were employed. If there were six ploughs on the field and six stetches then it worked out easily: each man did one round (two furrows) on every stetch, making up the twelve furrows – or, to be more exact, eleven furrows and the *brew* or *moul' furrow*. The *brew* was

*A judge: he uses upright sticks to estimate the straightness of the furrow.

very important as it completed or *shut up* the work. We called ploughing the last furrow in a stetch *taking up the brew*. In twelve-furrow work, or any narrow-stetch work for that matter, it was important that all the brews lay in one direction. If they didn't, the width of the stetches wouldn't be exact; and the drill and so on wouldn't fit the stetch; there was a waste of land or a waste of seed-corn. And if that happened you might as well hide your head in the hedge.

'The first baiter had a responsible job when he had a field full of ploughs to look after. He was a kind of foreman; and he had continually to be looking at his watch and calculating whether they were forrard enough. And as they came towards the end of the day he had to do some quick thinking to find out whether he'd have to keep the men working right up to the last minute in order to get the stint, of three-quarter of an acre's ploughing for each man, finished.

'After they gave up twelve-furrow work – when the machines came in – they went in for *flat-work*, wide stetches, even on the heaviest land, of anything up to eighteen yards. Then each man ploughed his own stetch after the first baiter had laid the top. That system was better in a way. It kept you on your toes. As soon as you had a break in your ploughing you'd walk along the *headlings* to have a look at your neighbour's work, to see where he had gone wrong, or if his ploughing was better than yours. It wouldn't do just to have straight furrows: a good ploughman also had to have a good *top* to the stetch – the furrows lying all flat and even. If there was a bit of *low* in the land, he had to let his plough bite in a little deeper at this spot to bring his furrows up level. You had to have level furrows as the drill *coulters** had to enter the land at equal depth everywhere. Some say: "Oh, don't worry about that! The harrows will level it off when they go over it." But the harrows would never level off. You can pick out a furrow after the harrow has gone over it. If a first baiter knew his job, as soon as a man had ploughed a stetch he'd drop his stick across the furrows. If the stick didn't lie flat, but went all *tittymatawta* (like a seesaw), he then wanted to know the reason for it. It was *work* in the days I'm telling you about. Now, if you see a ploughed field today, it looks exactly as if a lot of pigs have been a-hoggin' and a-rootin' on it up.'

A *level-top*, apart from its looking well, was emphasized for a good economic reason: if the ploughland was level, the drill coulters would bite in at an uniform depth, and sow the seed in the same way; the ears of corn would then mature at approximately the same time and all the seeds of corn would be approximately the same size. This was a big point in a barley-grower's favour when he took some of his corn to show to a maltster. For one of the first things the maltster looked for was just this: uniformity of seed in the samples that the farmer showed to him.

A ploughing match

'My father tied with another man at an Old Newton furrow-drawing match: both had a quarter-inch *deviation* – it must have been about sixty years ago. Now he had one peculiarity when he was a-ploughin': he had to have his pipe going before he could

*The metal 'spouts' down which the seed from the drill runs into the soil; often called *counters* in the dialect.

start. So this particular day at Old Newton, just before he started, he stopped to do the usual: get a good light on his owd pipe. One of the stewards saw him a-doin' this and he say:

'"Hurry up there! We're waiting for you to start. You can't smoke and draw a furrow at the same time."

'"Dew you be quiet. I know what I'm a-dewin' on."

'So he lit up his owd bit of clay pipe, put his hands to the plough and went after his horses. When he had drawn a furrow that everybody could see was one of the best – even before the *stickers* put the sticks on it – they say:

'"See! It's child's play for him. He smokes at it as if he's just a-digging' in his own garden!"

'They didn't know that he couldn't have drawn a proper furrow let alone a real good 'un if he hadn't got his owd pipe a-drawin' in his mouth! It just shows you: what you're used to, you must do – even if it's in a competition.'

ARTHUR CHAPLIN

Sowing the seed

The care given to the sowing of the barley by the East Anglian husbandman was almost akin to veneration. No trouble was spared to ensure that the carefully prepared seed-bed was ready to take the crop. One old farmer in the Stowmarket area of Suffolk said that, ideally, for the barley (and the wheat) crop the land should be ploughed east to west and then drilled *overwart* (athwart) so that the *ringes* or rows of young corn would lie north–south and be warmed by the sun on both sides of the row. But he would not sow until he was perfectly sure that the land was fit for drilling. He had his time-proven tests for this: one was simply to walk over the land and to 'feel it through his boots'; then again he would take up a handful of soil, carefully crumbling it to test it; or he would bend down and draw his fist backwards through the soil. This method of deciding the right time to sow was recommended by Fitzherbert, the sixteenth-century writer on agriculture: 'go upon the land that is plowed and if it synge or crye or make any noise under they fete, then it is to wet to sowe. And if it make no noyse and will bear thy horses, thanne sowe in the name of Godd.'

Some Suffolk husbandmen – up to the end of the last century, at least – took the advice to 'Go upon the land' in a very literal sense indeed. The husbandman's argument appears to have been this: he could easily determine by the above methods whether the seed-bed was ready for the corn and whether the soil was of the right tilth: but he could not be sure that the soil was warm enough to allow the seed to germinate. Therefore to make sure of this important condition he took off his trousers and sat down on the seed-bed, thus testing the warmth of Mother Earth through the most sensitive part of his anatomy. The writer has collected three instances of this practice: two in the Stowmarket district and one near Mendlesham where the farmer who recalled it made the comment after the cold and wet spring of 1963: 'I don't know how those owd bors who used to set on the seed-bed would get on today: I reckon they'd get themselves right chilled.' But the test was, apparently, extremely effective: for if after this exercise the ground was judged right and the sowing proceeded satisfactorily, the husbandman expected the barley 'to be up in three days'.

Good Friday in East Anglia used to be the traditional day for planting potatoes. It is difficult to say whether this was a fertility belief or whether this day was chosen simply because Good Friday was usually a holiday for the old farming community and therefore a convenient occasion for a workman to plant his own

[55]

garden. It is likely, however, that there is some element of the old belief in the practice, as this day was specially chosen in many English counties, notably Devon: 'By many people potatoes are planted on Good Friday afternoon; in south Devon it was said: "We sow our potatoes at the foot of the Cross".' The basis of the Good Friday belief appears to have been that on that day the soil is redeemed from the power of Satan – the old chthonic god of the pre-Christian religion – and for this brief time he has no influence on it at all.

Weeding

Under the old farming of pre-machine days a good test of a man's farming skill was to observe whether his land was clean or foul with weeds. If he got on top of his weeds and successfully kept them under one could be sure he was a good farmer. This skill is well summarized in the saying: *Farm in front of your rubbish*; and a Blaxhall farmer, W. A. Peake, explained to me what was behind it:

'A good farmer sowed his seed so he could take his crop of corn before the rubbish came on. You had to be a good farmer to do that, a good practical farmer. And you wouldn't get the

knowledge out of a book. There was no short cut: farming was an art and few men had it unless they'd come by it the hard way. Out of the gentlemen who came into farming at that time [before mechanization] only about one in twenty could make it go: the others had to have a skilled man to manage the farm for 'em. But the skill has gone out of farming now. Today, if a man takes over a farm and gets into a muddle, he has the fertilizers, the sprays and the weedkillers – the whole lot to get him out of it.'

Bird-scaring

Before the appearance of the corn shoots the farmer employed children, both girls and boys, to scare off the birds: in October and November to guard the winter corn, in March and April to watch over the spring sowing. Many of the old people who did this job sixty and seventy years ago told me some of their experiences. They called the job *crow-keeping*, a phrase that Shakespeare used to describe it; some called it *bird-keeping* or *bird-tending* – keeping the birds off the newly sown land – while others referred to it simply as *rook-scaring*. But whatever birds were warned off the method of doing it was very much the same in the whole of East Anglia. As soon as it was light the farmer sent the child out into the fields; and there the child remained while it was still light. Mrs Celia Jay of Blaxhall gave me an account of how she went crow keeping at the end of last century:

'My father was a shepherd for Mr John Goddard of Tunstall; and I would go out to scare rooks and crows on Mr Goddard's fields. My father made me a pair of wooden clappers and I used to rattle these and call out:

> *Cadows and crows,*
> *Take care of your toes.*
> *For here come my clappers*
> *To knock you down back'uds.*
> *Holla ca-whoo! Ca-whoo!*

Here come a stone
To break your back-bone:
Here come the farmer with his big gun
And you must fly and I must run.
Holla ca-whoo! Ca-whoo!

[Cadows are jackdaws, a word used by Thomas Tusser in the sixteenth century.]

'It was very lonely work, and I was often perished with cold before the end of the day. If I stopped making a noise, someone from the farm would soon be along to see what I was doing.'

A contemporary of Mrs Jay, Dan Pilgrim of Helmingham, remembers one of his first jobs on the farm after he left school at the age of twelve. The farmer sent him to keep a flock of larks off a field that had just been set with winter corn: 'It was late November or early December; and when it got dark about half past four time I made my way back to the farm thinking my job was done. But the foreman sent me back, although it was already too dark to see the field let alone the larks. He wanted me to stay up in there until half past five – knocking off time. I started back to the field but I fetched on round and went home instead.'

TAKING THE HARVEST

The harvest contract

Under the old community the harvest was the climax of the rural year, not merely an incident in the more mechanical and depersonalized round on the farm as it has become today. The whole village was involved and there was a carefully laid down ritual which had long roots far back in medieval times. The first step was known as *Taking the Harvest*. This meant that the men on each farm, with the addition of certain seasonal workers like the company of sheep-shearers, agreed with the farmer to bring in the harvest on 'piecework' – so much per acre of crops; or perhaps they would contract to get the harvest in during the period of a month from the time they started; or instead of a month some agreements would state *Twenty Four Fine Days*.

Here is an actual contract for 'taking the harvest': it was drawn up at Grove Farm by old George Rope some time during the last quarter of the nineteenth century. The confusion of person in the first sentence is understandable as the contract was written out in Old George's hand; and as the sole contracting party on one side it was easier for him to write *my* than the more impersonal, if more accurate, *the master's* or some other third person equivalent.

We the undermentioned agree to cut and secure all the corn grown on the farm in a workmanlike manner to my satisfaction; make bottoms of stacks; cover up when required; hoe the turnips twice and turn or lift the barley once; turn the pease once – each man to find a gaveller. Should any man lose any time through sickness he is to throw back 2s. per day to the Company and receive account at harvest. Should any man lose any time through drunkenness he is to forfeit 5s. to the Company.

> Joe Levett
> Jas. Hammond
> R. French
> Jn. Keable
> Joe Row
> Samuel Ling

Allowances to each man:
> 1 Coomb of Wheat at 20s.
> 3 Bushels of Malt – gift
> 1 lb of Mutton to each man instead of dinner
> 2½ lbs of Mutton at 4d. a lb every Friday

David Ling, lad: To receive half as much as the other men make in their harvest and half their allowances

Boy Woodbridge: ½ Bushel of Malt: 2/6 a week during harvest
Boy Leggett: 3s. a week during harvest. 1 Bushel of Malt

92 acres at 6s. 6d.   £29. 18. 0
                                        2. 0
                                _____
                               £30. 0. 0

[60]

If, instead of 'piecework', the men contracted to get the harvest in by the end of a month, it meant that should they finish before that time they could then go to other jobs on the farm, drawing their usual wage whilst doing so. If, however, they were unlucky enough to meet wet weather and the harvest extended itself over the stated month, then they might well find themselves working in the fifth week without drawing any extra money. But if the farmer had agreed to insert the phrase 'Twenty Four Fine Days' in the contract instead of one month, the contract would operate on fine days only: on wet days the men would do their usual tasks about the farm, drawing their usual wage for those particular days.

According to the above agreement the six men, the lad and two boys worked for £30. Estimating that the harvest would take a month to gather, this worked out that each man averaged about £1 4s. a week in wages; but out of this he would have to pay his gaveller. Yet even when she had been paid he would still have about double his normal wage – ten shillings, or even less in this village when the contract was drawn up about eighty years ago; and there were the allowances in addition. The harvest worker certainly earned this double pay as he started working at five o'clock in the morning and finished at dusk.

Many of the terms in the contract need comment; a coomb is

equivalent to four bushels; 'to make bottoms of stacks' refers to the practice of building the stack off the ground on a low iron or wooden platform to prevent vermin from getting into the corn. The *gavellers* were usually women, wives of the harvest workers. Their job was to rake the mown corn into *gavels* or rows ready for carting. Corn that was not bound into *shuffs* (sheafs) was said to be *on the gavel*. 'Barley,' as Arthur Young noted, 'is everywhere in Suffolk mown and left loose, the neater method of binding in sheaves is not practised. The stubbles are *dew-raked* by men drawing a long iron-toothed rake.' A tool called a *shack-fork* – a fork with curved tines and an iron bow at the shoulder was used to gather the swathes of barley into gavels ready for pitching on to the wagons. A gaveller worked behind each wagon feeding the corn to two men – one on each side of the wagon – who did the *pitching* while another two men on top of the load received the corn and arranged it evenly. The man paid the gaveller about a shilling a day: if she had a young child to look after at the same time she would have to manage as best she could. Priscilla Savage remembers her mother telling her that she was placed down in the shade between two bundles of corn in an angle of the harvest field, and she was fed during the brief intervals her mother won from the gavelling.

Threshing and combines

'Yeh, yeh. We happened on some good 'uns, and we happened on some sort of funny ones when we goo round. There were some good uns, good owd fellers. But there were a lot o' poor farmers at that time o' day. They was poor men but they was good 'uns. But there was some on 'em, they wasn't any too good. There was a lot of 'em; and I told 'em: about the thrashing:

'"When it come to the last quarter of an hour, you want to have that last a long while!"

'They was always in a hurry, but they didn't do anything properly. And there was a rare lot of them. They didn't make owd bones. They didn't make owd bones! It was no good. When

[62]

you go arter a job like that, if you're doing as fast as what the machine will take it to do it properly, you can't force it. I very often wonder how they do as they do today. When we went thrashing we had to set our things level to do our work. Now they can take a combine, they go up-hill, down-hill, side-hill – any owd way, and away they goo! We must have been fules, you see, to have took all that trouble to level our things up!'

JIMFER THROWER

Threshing the corn was the farmer's real harvest, the culmination, as he would not get paid until the corn was in the sack after threshing. And there was a feeling of achievement at the close of a successful threshing, the real climax of a year for a farmer in the corn area.

I have transcribed Jimfer Thrower's account of his threshing experience, starting in 1893:

'The first day's threshing I done was for a man by the name of Rogers, Harry Rogers. I got ninepence for that. A man got one and eightpence, and threepence allowed for beer. My first job was pulling away *colder*,* and carting chaff. After a little while I went on to the drum with Mr Stevens' brother, Sid; and then I got a full man's money, one and eightpence, a lot o' money to take home then. I was somewhere about fourteen. We used to thrash in the winter-time: and then, of course, we had to do something else in the summer. That didn't go on all the year. We started in August and went on until the job was finished. Of course, we only got one thrashing set at that time o' day, you see; and we'd finish in March or the fore-part of April time.

'I became a *feeder*, feeding the corn into the thrashing-drum. It was a bit of a risky job. I got a fork stuck through my hand more than once: I got several tips off here and little stabs and one thing and another. But I didn't pay much regard to that: that were all in the day's work. There was a man I worked with – I done seven seasons along with him: and there wasn't so much as an angry word or *dammit* passed between us. Of course, we had to walk to work at that time o' day. We walked 108 miles one week, and we earned eightpence each for the week! ... That was about 1907 or '08. We walked from Little Thornham to Stearns of Shimpling; and we walked there for a week. We went there with a new cloth on the drum, as near as could be; and when we come away there wasn't a piece of it no bigger than your hand.

*The refuse of threshed corn – light ears, bits of straw, etc., rubbish piled up behind the drum. The chaff, like the husks of corn, was saved in bags.

Wind! Wet! I got wet and then I got dry! and we couldn't do this job because of the weather. And there were oak trees stood up there; and it snapped three of 'em off just like snapping a match. That was a rum wind!'

A great wind

'But, of course, you wouldn't recollect the heavy wind. That's about seventy-five years ago. Well, that was a lovely Saturday. On the Sunday morning that started – the wind started blowing. And that was a funny, funny wind that was! That blow scores of trees down: cattle, horses on the meadow, some on 'em. It just took 'em up like that, and took 'em across: some were lying in the ditch, some in the hedge. And I've been wanting to ask if they got a record o' that at Pulham St Mary. The parson there, the chapel parson, he went there; and it just lifted the roof off the chapel like that and killed him in the pulpit, blew in the wall. As dead as a doornail! That was in 1895.*

'It took all the stacks up – tons and tons – and simply took 'em up like that off the ground and scattered them over the fields. I know a man, Mr Pymar, Spencer Pymar who lives at Diss. His father sent him after an owd man somewhere to come hoom; and he had an owd pony. And the wind took him up pony and all, and plumped him up against the hedge.'

JIMFER THROWER

*Sunday 24 March 1895. George Dearle of Diss, a Baptist minister, was struck in the pulpit by falling masonry. His skull was fractured and he died the next day after 'the operation of trepanning was carried out' in Norwich hospital. The *Norfolk Chronicle and Norwich Gazette*, 30 March 1895.

The sickle

The sickle is one of the oldest surviving implements in farming, and is still used in Suffolk – in the Bures district – but for harvesting thyme for seed and not for corn. The earliest farmers fashioned the first sickles out of pieces of sharp flint fixed in a curved bone or piece of wood. Later the sickle was made from metal with a saw-edged or serrated blade. The reaper cut the corn by bending over and grasping a bunch of ears in his left hand, as Caleb Howe* did on his allotment, inserting the sickle and drawing it towards him in a sawing action. This was essentially a gentle action and it ensured that as little corn as possible would be shed and lost on the ground. The sickle lasted for so long as a harvesting tool for this very reason: it was still used in preference to the swap-hook and scythe in some areas because its use, although slower, conserved the grain.

Frank Bloomfield worked most of his life with Ransome, Sims and Jefferies the famous Ipswich firm of agricultural engineers; and he gave me a very modern illustration of this quality of a serrated edge. When his firm first experimented with making a combine-harvester, the blades they used on the cutter were smooth-edged like the swap-hook, or scythe, or the blades on a reaper-binder. But they found that a tremendous amount of grain was lost by being shed on to the stubble. The firm then

*Caleb Howe of Framsden (1886–1967) on the Helmingham estate. His allotment was a half-acre at the back of his cottage.

experimented by making one side of the cutting knives with serrated edges, leaving the other smooth-edged. This improved the performance of the combine-harvester slightly; but it was not until they had made serrated edges on all the knives that the loss of grain lessened appreciably. Thus the wheel has come full circle: the main feature in the design of the primitive sickle is included – much to its advantage – in the latest models of the combine harvester.

But the design of the old, serrated sickle was also outstanding in another way: it was light and could be used all day, even by women, without the reaper tiring unduly. The curve of the blade contributed greatly to this, as Henry Stephens showed in his *Book of the Farm*. Its long use down the ages had evolved the sickle's peculiar sweeping curve which gave the tool perfect balance, ensuring that it would need the minimum effort for its use. Stephens called it *the curve of least exertion*, a design that was mathematically perfect for the use to which it was put.

There were other reasons for the long use of the sickle. 'With it,' as Caleb Howe stated, 'you could cut your corn high. You couldn't do that with the scythe.' It was light enough for a woman to use; the scythe was a different matter. Lastly the serrated blade of the sickle required no sharpening: it would last for a whole harvest without attention. Therefore, although it was a little slower in use, no time was lost in the field through frequent breaks for sharpening with the rub-stone as were needed with both swap-hook and scythe.

Sickle and flail

George Messenger, a seventy-nine-year-old neighbour, worked at the nearby Snape Maltings. He told me how he worked his *candy** or piece of common-yard, dividing it into two by a path,

---

*I have been unable to find this word in the dialect dictionaries. It may have been a corruption of *cansey*: a causeway or footpath across a common, an acre of which had been enclosed.

and growing wheat on one side and vegetables on the other, changing over the crops each year. He cut the wheat with a serrated sickle.

'I bound up the wheat in little bunches. Then when it was thrashed I had a straw bed laid down nice and thick on the barn floor. And I got a *frail* and thrashed that. Then I'd take all the straw off the floor. There lay the wheat. I put it in a basket whatever I'd got and then dress it with a 'blower' or dressing machine (if I could borrow one). This would blow the chaff away. I remember the first time I used the *frail* I got a clout o' the skull that I'd remember. An old chap that was there said: "Never mind that, you'll get plenty o' those."'

Shacking

An old shepherd Harry Mason confirmed [the] shedding of the corn by the first combines: 'I used to turn my sheep out on to the corn stubble. We called it *shacking* [feeding on the corn that had been *shacked* or shaken out of the ear during harvest]. This was quite straightforward when they scythed the corn or used the self-binder: I could leave the sheep in the stubble for the best part of the day and I needn't worry much about them. But as soon as the combine came in I had to be very careful with them. They picked up so much more corn that – if I were to leave them – they'd have been in trouble in no time. They would be on their backs, legs in the air and their bellies all blown up. They'd get so much grain and they'd eat it so quickly that it swelled out before they had time to digest it. It was very easy to lose sheep like that. So after the combine had been I used to open the two gates to the field; let 'em in through one and drive 'em almost straight away out through the other.'

Gleaning

In the Blaxhall and Tunstall district earlier in the last century, the sexton used to ring the church bell at eight o'clock in the morning as a signal that the gleaning could start in the parish. He rang it again at seven o'clock at night to warn the gleaners that their work for that day must end. But during living memory farmers used the following practice to control the gleaning and to prevent forestalling and argument among the gleaners. After the farm-workers had cleared a field of the crop they left one sheaf standing on it. This last sheaf was called the *Policeman*, and it was understood that no gleaner could enter the field while the Policeman was on guard. As soon as the farmer took the last sheaf away the gleaners were free to enter.

The conditions of the farm-workers during the 1890s made gleaning essential: a loss of the gleaned corn would have meant

actual hunger to many a farm-worker's family during the ensuing year. This is the reason why the school authorities realized it would be useless to open school while the gleaning was still in progress.

Riding the goaf

Barns were a vital part of the economy in the corn areas, a focus of much of the work. Moreover, the outstanding East Anglian barns like the Paston barn near North Walsham in Norfolk or the Framsden Hall barn in Suffolk, show how important these old farm buildings are from the standpoint of medieval architecture. Some of them are constructed very much like a church; and an Essex writer, C. Henry Warren, very aptly called them 'cathedrals of labour'. When empty the ten-bay Framsden barn, and even more so the Paston barn which is built of stone, have the same noble proportions as the nave of a great church.

But the small farm barns have usually only three bays, each about fifteen to sixteen feet across; and this too is the usual width of the actual barn itself.

Big double doors led to the central bay of the barn, the middlestead, where the threshing was later carried on. The double doors allowed the wagons loaded with corn to pass right through on to the floor of the middlestead. The men then unloaded the corn into the side bays each of which was called the *gof* – or *goafstead*. Gof or gove means the corn in the ear or the *mow* or stack; that is, before it is threshed. Tusser called it the *goef*, and we can be sure that, like the word, the design of the barn itself and the work that went on in it had hardly changed from the sixteenth century to within living memory.

One practice linked with this stage of the harvest was called *riding the goaf* in Suffolk. As the loose barley was unloaded on to the goafstead, a boy rode a quiet old farmhorse round and round on the corn, trampling it down. The main purpose was to pack as much corn as possible into the bay; but in treading the corn in this way much of it was shaken out of the ear, and thus a start was made on the threshing. Many of the older Suffolk farm-workers, now long retired, remember riding the goaf as lads; and they have described how they rose higher and higher on the mow as it increased in depth. The problem came when horse and rider could rise no higher and had to be got down. One man told me that they left a rough sort of ramp at one side of the corn, and the horse slid down this on to the middlestead. Another described how a strong rope was thrown over one of the barn's tie-beams and then fixed to the horse's harness. The men then eased him down by taking much of his weight on the rope.

gof - or goafstead   middlestead   gof - or goafstead

Machines

Abraham Ling, a farm-worker from Blaxhall, told me about 1950, and I recorded his remarks a little later:

'It's the machines! They'll hev to come back to hosses yet. Two ton of iron [the tractor] going over the land don't do it no good – it stands to reason! You git the roller on the land, it's true; but too much of that ain't no use. It's inways and sideways: thet's how they go on with the land today. It's not done. It's got over.'

THE HORSE

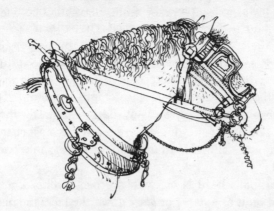

Names of horses

In an old catalogue of a farm and stock, sold in Blaxhall in the year 1812 the following names of horses are included: Dodman, Jolly, Diment (Diamond?), Smiler, Depper and Darby. The cows had names like Gypsy, Violet, Nancy (or Bud); while the more poetic ones were Whiteface, Clowdy and Gardy-good or Gather-good. Some of the village children took the trouble not long ago to collect the present-day names of the animals on the farms. They compared them with the names on the above catalogue and with those on two other farm catalogues, one dated 1873, the other 1919. The first of these had the following names for horses: Boxer, Matchet, Dapper, Scot (a name with a lineage at least as old as Chaucer), Diamond, Darby, Sharper, Captain, Proctor, Briton, Smiler, Dragon, Doughty, Gyp, Moggy. The cows were Cherry, Brindy and Cowslip. There were only cows' names in the 1919 catalogue. They were Snape, Violet, Comly, Cherry and Strawberry. The children found that many of the old names had been kept but naturally a number of new ones, such as Frisky, Fay, Titania and Babs, had crept in. The newest of all was a cow's name – Mercedes.

The Suffolk punch

What are the main characteristics of the Suffolk breed of horse? The first and obvious one is the clearly defined colour. The colour of the old breed was distinguished by the now obsolete term sorrel* – a name which still remains in many Suffolk inns. The colour today is chesnut;† but there are seven shades of chesnut: the red; the golden; the lemon or yellow; the light, mealy chesnut; the dark; the dull-dark, and lastly the bright chesnut. The bright chesnut is considered the most characteristic colour and, all other things being equal, the one to be preferred.

The Suffolk's head is big with a broad forehead, and often with a star on it or a *shim*‡ or *blaze* down the face; the neck deep in the collar and tapering to a graceful setting of the head; the shoulders long and muscular and thrown well back at the withers. The well-rounded rib – the barrel chest that has helped to give the Suffolk the name of Punch – is a distinctive feature, as is the deep carcase. This last is one of the first essentials of a true Suffolk; for it was bred for use on the farm, and for use on the Suffolk farms in particular, where it was the custom for the horses to work a long day from 6.30 a.m. to 2.30 p.m. without nosebag or any break for rations. An ample *bread-basket* was thus indispensable to the Suffolk; and this characteristic – emphasized by selective breeding – is another example of the inspired fusion of breed, local custom and use that has gained East Anglian farmers such a deserved reputation as stock raisers.

The shapely outline of back loin and quarters is as noticeable as the deep carcase. 'Feet, joints and legs – the legs should be straight with fair, sloping pasterns, big knees and long clean hocks on short cannon bones, free from coarse hair; the feet

---

Sorrel was the name of the horse that tripped over a mole-hill and fatally threw William III.

†This spelling is the traditional rendering wherever the word is linked with the Suffolk horse.

‡*shim*: a white mark, a dialect word from OE *scima* – brightness or splendour.

should have plenty of size with circular form protecting the frog; walk, smart and true; trot – well balanced all round with good action. If one were asked the question what are the four chief characteristics of the Suffolk horse? the answer would certainly be – colour, quality, compactness and hardy constitution.'*

Master ploughman

My main Scottish informant, Norman Halkett a farmer's son, born in 1910 in Huntly, Aberdeenshire, sketched in his own background and his early involvement with horses:

'I was a child when I learned other things also. For instance, how to groom a horse, how to harness it and how to walk up and down the long rigs alongside your favourite ploughman, listening to his songs and watching his work with the horses. The great art among them was to make a pair of horses plough with no reins at all, to finish the rig, turn the horses and commence another rig – still with no reins. When evening came, or rather when *lousing-time* came (lousing-time was when the day's work was over and the horses were *loosened* from the yoke), they were then handed over more or less to us children. We were placed on top of the leading beast; and our art was to bring them home by words only, no reins to be used. They turned this way and that to *hie* or *wheesh* or *tcht tcht* or *whoa*; and of course, I have no doubt the horses were so tired they would have found their way home any way. But we children thought we too were master horsemen.

'The love and affection which these ploughmen or horsemen

*Raymond Keer, 'The Suffolk Horse,' *M & B Veterinary Review*, November 1952.

had for their animals was quite extraordinary. They groomed them; they fed them; they looked after them in every way as a mother would look after her son. And I have seen them at the mid-day rest hour of twelve to one, I have seen a ploughman come into the stable, shake up the straw in the stall of his leading beast and lie down there and sleep. I've seen the man's face actually resting on the foot of the horse; but never at any time the horse stand on him, tramp on him or damage him in any way. You'd think there'd be fear that the ploughman would suffer damage among the horse's hoofs, but such was the bond between them that nothing of the kind ever happened.'

The gentleness of heavy horses

'We used to go down to the park on Sunday afternoons, taking the children down when they were very young. He'd whistle and all the horses would run over to us; and there we were surrounded by these great horses, and we were holding up the babies to them! It scares me now just to think of it. But they were very gentle. My husband was ploughing once and he told me: "Stand in the furrow." And he set the plough, let go the handles and walked alongside the horses as they ploughed. The horses drew right up to me before they stopped. On another occasion I was sitting on a bank with my feet on the headland, and Walter was coming along with his horses. I drew my feet in naturally to let them pass, but he called out: "No, leave your feet there!" Sure enough, the horses stepped gently over my feet without touching them.'

MRS LILIAN CATER

A shining coat

To make the coat shine each horseman had his own, usually secret, recipe. One used tansy leaves: 'You dried them and then rubbed them atween your hands. You kept this powder in a little linen bag and you sprinkled a bit now and then in their bait.' Another used sweet saffron leaves, baked to dry and fed in the same way: 'Only you had to be some careful not to give the horse too much of the powder or else the sweat would bring it out and you could smell the herb on his coat.' Another horseman used bryony root – a fairly common remedy in Suffolk: 'Bryony is a big root like a passnip. You cut it up: let it dry, and feed it with the chaff.' One horseman knew bryony as *big-root*: 'We used to come across it while we were ditching. I used to borrow my wife's nutmeg grater and then I'd grate up some of the root and feed it to 'em with the chaff.' One horseman asserted that the best device to make the coat shine was to wet the chaff occasionally with a little urine.

Dobbin's straw bonnet

'Well then, if it was a summer thing that was going he'd be put in full show regalia; and that was with his bonnet on his head. It was a straw bonnet, biscuit-coloured and it was worked round the edges with red; I suppose it was thin cord; but it had red round it and red on the top. And he would take one ear and then the other ear and pull it through the slots on the bonnet. Then when he'd got the bonnet firmly on Dobbin's head, he'd get some little coverings for the ear – to keep the flies off. They were like little nets: they were exactly the shape of a horse's ears: he pulled them down over the ears, and they each had a red or blue tassel hanging on them. Then, of course, he had a cover for keeping the flies off. That was also – I think it must have been a very heavy string net; and that also had down each side, very long red or blue tassels. And then his socks [leg hair]: he had beautiful white socks all round his fetlocks. And they were combed until they shone.'

MRS G. REYNOLDS

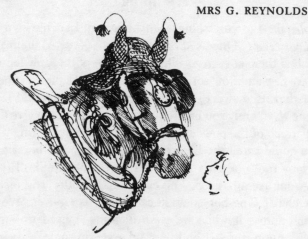

Braid and ribbons

As well as being very particular about the horses' condition the old horsemen were equally concerned about their appearance. Their coats had to shine like satin, and their harness had to be in as good condition as possible. They also had to be decorated with braid and ribbons even when they were out ploughing in the winter; George Sadler told me:

'We had to get into the stable very early in the morning to feed and braid up the horses. It took an hour and a half to braid properly. You always had to do the tails up summer-fashion or winter-fashion. There was never a horse went out unless that tail was done up. It had to be left long with just a little braid on the top and twisted underneath with a little bit of straw through for the summer. And the whole lot would be done up from the bottom as a winter "do-up" to stop the mud from getting on to it.'

Charles Rookyard's stallion

Breeding and sex in general were a part of the natural order of things to the people of the old farming community; and this is another aspect of it that reminds us of its ancient roots. It is exactly the same attitude as we find in Chaucer's *Canterbury Tales*; and it is no exaggeration to say that a Suffolk stallion leader, like Charles Rookyard, was in direct line with the carter in *The Friar's Tale*. Like him he called one of his horses *Scot*: like him, too:

> *This carter thakketh [pats] his horse upon the croupe [rump]*
> *And they begonne drawen and to-stoupe*

in exactly the same way as the Suffolk Punch would get down or stoop on to its knees in its efforts to draw a full or heavy load. And his attitude to breeding and increase was as matter-of-fact as that of some of the pilgrims who went to Canterbury in the fourteenth century. This comes out in Charles Rookyard's description of an incident when he was leading his stallion, *Sudbourne Benedict*, around some of the farms in the Helmingham district:

'I once met a parson when I was travelling with an entire horse* and he said:

' "Hullo! Good morning, young fellow."

'I said: "Good morning, sir."

' "I would love," he said, "to go along with you just to see this horse do the work."

' "Well," I said, "there's nothing to stop you. I'm now a-going to Mr Gooding's, straight to his farm, Redhouse, Witnesham. You can come if you like. There's nothing wrong about that."

*A stallion.

[79]

'"Well," he said, "I would like to come. Do you drink beer?" I said: "That I do. That's just one of my main points."

'"All right," he said, "I'll go and get a bottle," and he went and got a bottle of ale and brought one out for himself. I thought to myself, "You got good religion in you, and this is better than drinking tea."

'So he brought my bottle out and poured his out and we tapped glasses together. He says:

'"Here's good luck."

'I said: "Thank you very much, sir."

'And he said: "I'll come on with you."

'So he came up to the farm, and they had a job for my horse, which he was very interested in. And when I started back, he said:

'"Are you coming back past mine?"

'I said: "Yes, sir."

'"Well, we'll have another drink. Can you drink another?"

'"Sure," I said, "that would be just my hobby."

'He said he never was so surprised in his life. He never thought anything like that would happen.

'"Yes, sir," I said. "That's nature with a horse, just the same as there's nature with the human beings."

'And what his idea was, in a way I suppose, was just to see the position which I had to get the horse into before he had the job with the mare; and he wondered how the job was done with the harness I'd got on. But I used to take all the harness off, hold the horse back, and I said, "Right!" and the job was done.'

There we have in one of its aspects the likeness of the old country society that has just passed away to the society described by Chaucer: a cool, matter-of-fact treatment of a subject that could have so many overtones. To Chaucer, as to the old countryman, what we might regard as broad or even bawdy is a plain fact of nature, as neutral or objective as – to use Chaucer's own word – the engendring of the simple flower.

Mervyn Cater's drill

In recounting his early lessons on the farm Mervyn Cater illustrates what a high standard of craftsmanship meant, not only in horse matters but in general work on the farm: and what kudos and local reputation the highest standard gave to the horseman. His father had decided while his son was still very young to give him instruction in using a steerage-drill, a machine to drill or sow the corn: this was an operation that demanded a high degree of skill and also care not to jeopardize one's own reputation because any mistake one made in the drilling would be visible to all when the crop came up. It was a Smythe drill, and his father took him on some 'short work', a piece of land where no one could see it. He was allowed to drive the drill backwards and forwards for a couple of dozen times. His father walked beside him, behind him, leaned on him, did everything he could to teach him to drill. One day, after he had been having lessons for some time, his father was called away by the boss: there was a horse in the ditch: it had gone to sleep on the edge and had rolled upside down into the ditch and couldn't get out. They came and took his father away to help with this horse. Mervyn was left with the drill:

'I stood beside the drill and kept looking up at this line we had just made; and it was like a gun-barrel. It must be easy once it was straight! (I got a bent line if I did it on my own, but here was one to follow.) It looked so easy to walk along that straight line; and of course it was a long field right to the road. In the end I had to have a go! I walked round the back to the drill put the lever on and let the corn run, and I drive those horses across the field. When I looked back that was dreadful. That was inches out. I turned the horses round, kept them on the headland and didn't drill any more that day. When my father seen this he was hurt – not angry, he was hurt!'

He was hurt because the reputation he prized, perhaps most of all, of being an all-round expert on the farm would now be jeopardized: and when Walter Cater met the horseman he admired most in the district, as he did every Sunday morning, he was asked quite seriously: 'What! Were you taken ill, Walter?' And although his father said: 'It was thet boy o' mine!', the bent drill-furrow was always a source of leg-pulling between the two friendly rivals: 'You're not a'going to tell me a tale like thet, Walter Cater. You fell over! Course you did.'

The working day

At eleven o'clock the teams stopped working. The horseman threw a couple of sacks over the backs of his horses and sat under the hedge to eat his *elevenses*. The break lasted twenty minutes; but it was not a complete break for the horseman for he was still in charge of the horses; and as they were not feeding they sometimes got restless, especially in the summer-time when the flies worried them and sometimes caused a horse to get his foot over a trace. Even when he was resting the horseman had to be on the alert for incidents like this to see that nothing untoward happened to his team. After the break he resumed work and continued until two-thirty in the afternoon when it was the end of the day as far as the horses were concerned.

But why this peculiar organization of the horseman's day which to a large extent cut across the hours of the other workers on the farm? The answer appears to be that such was the traditional day for the ploughman from time immemorial when his team was made up solely of oxen. Medieval records show that the oxen ploughed only in the morning and returned to their stalls shortly after mid-day. The old Welsh laws, dating from the middle of the tenth century, make it clear that the oxen were not to be used in the afternoon; and as Seebohm points out a *cyvar* (or co-ploughing, where different people contributed different members of the ox-team and the plough itself) ended at noon.

But why start early and finish in the middle of the day? Plough-ing was particularly burdensome to the oxen during the heat of the day, and by finishing at noon they would escape the greater part of it. But an important reason for the long, unbroken stretch of work in the field was undoubtedly the amount of time and trouble that was necessary to yoke and unyoke a team of eight, or even four, oxen. A break during the middle of the day and a return to the stables – apart from the question of distance from the field where the work was being done – would have meant unyoking and yoking up a second time for another stint in the afternoon; and this would have lengthened the day without appreciably lengthening the working time. Therefore it was natural that the ploughing should be done in one extended visit to the field: it was convenient that this should fall in the forepart of the day while the afternoon was spent, by the oxen in resting, and by their driver and ploughman in feeding them and seeing to their wants.

That the traditional shape of the old horseman's day was a continuation of the much older discipline submitted to by the ox-driver and the ploughman is borne out by some of the terms

that still survive in Suffolk. One old horseman put forward his opinion that the reason for the teams' long stretch of work in the early part of the day was, in fact, to save *taking off* (the harness etc.) in the middle of the day; and – what is more interesting – he referred to the day's visit to the field as a *journey*. In medieval times the acre or strip, which was the average day's ploughing for an ox-team, was sometimes called a *jurnalis* (or *diurnalis*) in monks' Latin and *journel* in French – that is, the amount of ploughing that could be done in one day.

HORSE MAGIC

Horse magic

The farm, it has been said, is the last resort of magic. This is probably true; but we can now see that we must not interpret this word *magic* too uncritically. For it is part of magic's function to conceal its real dynamic under a smoke-screen of fustian and fantasy, precisely because magic is no longer magic if it ceases to be the monopoly of the class or section who practise it. A secret that is shared by the whole community has no realizable value, and brings no kudos – of status or actual economic advantage.

Jading a horse

One of the most interesting and spectacular devices of the old farm horsemen was the stopping of a horse dramatically so that it would not move. This was called in East Anglia *jading* a horse; and it was from this practice more than any other that the horsemen sometimes earned the name of *horse-witches* because they were able to make the horse stand as though it were paralysed or bewitched. A note in Gibbon shows how ancient this practice was. It concerns the sixth-century Gothic king, Clovis:

'After the Gothic victory, Clovis made rich offerings to St Martin of Tours. He wished to redeem his warhorse by the gift of one hundred pieces of gold, but the enchanted steed could not move from the stable till the price of his redemption had been doubled. This *miracle* provoked the king to exclaim: *Vere, B. Martinus est bonus in auxilio, sed carus in negotio.*'* (Indeed, St Martin may be a good friend when you're in trouble, but he's an expensive one to do business with.) It is evident that the priests who served St Martin knew how to jade a horse and to attribute its state to the saint's intervention; and if Gibbon had had the slightest suspicion of how the *miracle* had been performed he would have used a much stronger form of irony than a mere italicizing of the word itself. For the priests, in fact, were doing exactly the same trick, and probably by exactly the same means, as the old East Anglian and Scottish horsemen who made out and actually believed that the horse's immobility was the result of some secret and magical device they had resorted to. This incident concerning the saint is also an example of early Christianity's adaptation of the old pagan beliefs, with politic foresight, for its own purpose; and, as already shown, traces of the sacred horse-cult remained in Christian ceremony for centuries after this event recorded by Gibbon.

A later instance of the practice of jading a horse is quoted by Margaret Murray:†

'Another man-witch, who was sentenced to the galleys for life, said that he had such a pity for the horses which the postillion galloped along the road that he did something to prevent it, which was that he took vervain and said over it the *Pater Noster* five times and the *Ave Maria* five times, and then put it on the road so that the horses should cease to run.'

A more recent instance comes from the Suffolk village of Polstead‡ towards the end of the last century: this shows also the same identification of the practice with witchcraft:

*Decline and Fall of the Roman Empire, vol. VI, ch. 38.
†*The God of the Witches*, p. 154.
‡Mrs Kate Rose (born 1881 at Polstead).

'A harvest wagon was coming in from the field when suddenly the horses stopped and refused to go any further. Then someone suggested beating the wheels of the wagon with branches of broom. But still the horses wouldn't budge: they were fixed as if something was holding them to the road. They didn't move either until they got one of the old horsemen: he got them away without any trouble.' The broom plant, it may be noted, was supposed to possess magical qualities as well as being a useful implement at home: the broom stick – that is, the green broom – could sweep out a room or carry a witch. The broom, according to the witch tradition, could give or blast fertility. Mrs Leather gave a similar instance of jading a horse from Herefordshire* but without deducing anything from it except that the old woman concerned was thought to be a witch.

The following example of horse jading happened in Suffolk just after the First World War. It is typical of how an older horseman† who had in his possession most of the ancient

*The Folklore of Herefordshire.
†William Charles Rookyard, the stallion leader, cf. p. 79.

secrets, was able to deal with a situation that had baffled a younger man. The older horseman tells the story:

'I was coming home with three lovely black horses which we always used on the road; and I used to glory in trimming them up, because they wore the worsted – red, white and blue – and they used to look lovely. I found I'd come to the Wetherden *Maypole*, and there was a chap there with his horses. He said to me:

'"Hullo, Charlie. You're just the chap I want to see."

'I said: "What's the matter now, mate?"

'"Somebody's been *a-doing the saddle up* on my horses and I cannot get these horses away. The trace-horse is backing and the *fill'us** is going another way!"

'"Wait here a minute, bo'," I said; "I'll tell you what: you've been a-braggin' again, haven't you?"

'"No," he says, "I haven't said a lot."

'"I told you," I said, "you must not brag what you can do, because there's allus somebody as good a man as yourself. Here now," I said, "wait a minute . . ."

'"What about your horses?" he said.

'"I ain't frightened my horses will run away: it's yours I'll have to look after."

'So I just went a-front there with my milk and vinegar; rubbed it in my palm and fingers; and then I rubbed it inside the horses' nose and then round their nostrils. I then said to this young horseman: "Now hop on your wagon and be off!" and he done so.'

As can be inferred from the above account there is no magical practice involved. Someone had played a trick on the young horseman and had put down a substance that was so obnoxious to the horses' delicate sense of smell that they would not move. The older and more knowledgeable horseman knew exactly what had happened and took immediate steps to neutralize this smell. The substance or substances were placed down either on an object in front of the horse or somewhere on the front of the

*The shaft-horse.

horse himself. Until the smell of the substance is neutralized the horse will not move forward an inch, resisting all kinds of persuasion and even force. One horseman revealed that he could jade a horse standing, say, on the sandy apron outside an inn simply by walking round him and unobtrusively dropping one of the obnoxious powders in the sand, especially in front of him: 'You didn't have to touch the horse, but that would stop him.' The same horseman also revealed that if this particular device had been used there was no need to use a neutralizing substance. A well-informed horseman simply had to grasp the horse's head firmly and give it a sharp turn and *back* him out of the area that had been contaminated by the jading substance.

One cunning old horseman used to jade a horse simply by pretending to feel the horse's fetlocks, but with the palm of his hand covered with the repellent substance. Later when he wanted to release him he had only to go through the same motion but this time having his hand covered with a substance that would neutralize the smell. And he gulled, and also impressed, the bystanders by lifting up one of the horse's front hoofs, giving it two or three sharp taps with his knuckles and saying confidently: 'Right! He'll go now.'

Many of these secret jading substances are organic; and their number is added to by, for instance, an observant horseman adapting something for his own use. While out ploughing a horseman had noticed a stoat some distance away stalking a rabbit. The stoat was gradually moving round unobserved by the rabbit. But as soon as the stoat got into the wind and the rabbit scented it, the rabbit set up a shriek and remained as though paralysed. It was easy then, as the horseman saw, for the stoat to make its kill. The incident remained in his mind and was reinforced by another experience he had shortly afterwards. He was ploughing a stetch not far from the headlands when his two horses suddenly stopped dead. He was too wise and experienced a horseman to attempt to force them to go forward: instead he turned them short and proceeded to plough another stetch. A little while later he gave his horses a rest, and returned to the spot they had refused to pass. He found a dead stoat lying near the hedge. Reasoning from this he made himself a jading substance compounded of stoat's liver and rabbit's liver, dried and powdered up and added to *dragon's blood** which was a code name among the old horsemen for one of their more powerful jading substances. The same horseman, a stallion-leader, gave another instance of how he made use of the horse's hyper-sensitive power of smell. When his horse staled he kept some of the urine. He corked it down in a bottle until the smell was particularly aggressive. If he wanted to keep his horse away from a certain mare he had only to rub some of the liquid on the stallion's bridle or on the mare to ensure that the horse would not go near her.

Drawing a horse

In addition to the repellent or jading substances there are the *drawing* or *calling oils*. They have the opposite effect: they *draw* or *call* a horse towards the horseman; but they, too, depend for their effect on the horse's keen sense of smell. The drawing oils are nearly all aromatic oils to which the horse is attracted. The following will show how the name *drawing* arose. To catch a frisky horse or a young colt in a field the horseman placed a little of the mixture of oil of origanum, oil of rosemary, oil of cin-

---

*The actual substance is red-gum resin which exudes from a kind of palm-fruit.

namon, and oil of fennel about his person. The instructions with this recipe which came from an old horseman's notebook were: *Set this mixture by the wind*; that is, the horseman was advised to stand in the wind so that as soon as the colt or horse scented him he would advance towards him. On a warm day, the instructions said, it would be sufficient for the horseman to place a few drops on his perspiring forehead to *call* his horses from a fair distance without saying a word, or making any sound.

Another device was to bake sweet-scented cakes to give to the horse as tit-bits:

'*It is For Catching Wild Colts and Vicious Horses on Aney Feild or Common* (For a long distance)
You must get by the wind and take with you scented cakes made as follows: half lb of oat flower mixed with Treacle and slack baked. Then sweat it under your arms. The cakes to be scented with the oil of origanum, oil of cinnamon, oil of fennel, the oil of rosemary and the oil of vidgin. If you have not time to bake the cakes you must scent a peice of gingerbread and give him that, and it will answer the same purpose.'

The castor or wart that grows on the inside of a horse's foreleg was also used as the basis for a drawing powder:

'Dry it in your pocket; great it into powder with a bright file or rasp. And it will be a pure white powder. Put it in a verey Close Box for the purpose. This powder has a great attraction for all animals, and the horse itself. The oil of rhodium possesses peculiar properties: all animals cherish a fondness for it and it exercises a subduing influence over them. Oil of Cumin: the horse has an instinctive passion for this. Both are natives of Arabia. With this knowledge horse taming becomes easy, and when the horse scents the odour he is drawn toward it.'

Drawing oils and jading substances were sometimes used with spectacular effect. A Norfolk man answered an advertisement for a horse-leader in Essex. He went down to the farm and applied for the job. They told him that the horse's previous leader – an old man – had died suddenly. He asked to see the horse and they took him to the stable. When he got to the horse's stall he found it was locked. Then the farmer admitted that there had been many applicants for the job already, but each had been driven out of the stall by the horse. Latterly they had been feeding him by dropping his fodder from a loft above the stall, and lowering down pails of water on a string. The farmer warned him of the danger of entering the stall. But the Norfolk man said: 'Never mind. Give me the keys.' He opened the door, took off his cap and threw it into the stall: 'If that's welcome,' he said, 'so am I.' In a short time the horse came to the door: they put the bridle on him and shortly afterwards the Norfolk man was taking the horse to the smithy to be shod. A similar incident happened in the Hartest district of Suffolk. A vicious stallion had 'got the master' of his leader who could not do anything with him. Someone sent for the narrator's father: 'My father said: "I'll come later on tonight: I'll catch him for you." They couldn't catch this stallion: it was in a loose box and it got on top of the chap who'd been leading it. The chap had tried but he daren't tackle him any longer. That night my father went out after it, but he did something before he left. As soon as he got to the loose box where they had the horse he pulled a little bit of stick about six inches long out of his pocket and threw it right up into the manger. The horse went up to the manger and stood there. Then my father went in and put his headstall on and led him out. But he never did tell me what he'd put on that stick.'

The Water of the Moon

In the writer's experience of recording the practices of old farm horsemen the frog's or toad's bone was nearly always linked with the jading of a horse, and they used the repellent substances with the bone, which was either powdered or whole, in this practice. Like the milt* it has wide and ancient associations. Here is a description by a Norfolk horseman of his way of getting and preparing the toad's bone. It is unusual for two reasons: he used the powdered bone of the toad with drawing oils and substances instead of with jading substances as most horsemen in Suffolk did; again, the description of the actual ritual of getting with all the attendant circumstances is of the deepest interest. He described the whole process as *The Water of the Moon*, presumably referring to its happening in a running stream when the moon was at the full:

'Well, the toads that we use for this are actually in the Yarmouth area in and around Fritton. We get these toads alive and bring them home. They have a ring round their neck and are what they call *walking toads*.† We bring them home, kill them, and put them on a whitethorn bush. They are there for twenty four hours till they dry. Then we bury the toad in an ant-hill; and

---

*The milt is a small oval lump of fibrous matter that lies on a foal's tongue when it is in the mare's womb. It was extracted by the horseman from the foal's mouth the moment it was born.

†The natterjack (*Bufo calamita*).

it's there for a full month, till the moon is at the full. Then you get it out; and it's only a skeleton. You take it down to a running stream when the moon is at the full. You watch it carefully, particular not to take your eyes off it. There's a certain bone, a little crotch bone it is, it leaves the rest of the skeleton and floats uphill against the stream. Well, you take that out of the stream, take it home, bake it, powder it and put it in a box; and you use oils with it the same as you do for the milch. While you are watching these bones in the water, you must on no consideration take your eyes off it. Do [if you do] you will lose all power. That's where you get your power from for messing about with horses, just keeping your eyes on that particular bone. But when you are watching it and these bones are parting, you'll hear all the trees and all the noises that you can imagine, even as if buildings were falling down or a traction engine is running over you. But you still mustn't take your eyes off, because that's where you lose your power. Of course, the noises must be something to do with the Devil's work in the middle of the night. I've been lucky enough to get two lots through, but with the third lot I didn't succeed. I think what really happened then [the third time] there was a sort of crackling in the noises as if someone was falling down. It makes you take your eyes off it. Then there was no answer: he [the bone] had no power. He wouldn't answer. But once you got the bone, you take it home, bake it, dry it well, and break it up into powder. You preserve it in a tin or bottle till you want it. Or you can mix it in the bottle with the oil so it's always handy in your pocket if you ever have occasion to use it. You put it on your finger, wipe the horse's tongue, his nostrils, chin, and chest – and he's your servant; you can do what you like with him.'

We shall return to the second part of the old horseman's description: here it is necessary to emphasize that he used it in an exceptional way. Most horsemen in Suffolk did not powder the bone but used it whole and also as a device to jade and not to draw the horse. They also went to a running stream at midnight at full moon, after going through the same procedure with the frog or toad. But after extracting the bone from the stream they cured it in jading substances. They then wrapped it in linen and concealed it about their person: to jade a horse they touched him in the pit of the shoulder with the frog's bone: to release the horse they touched him on the rump. The bone itself is probably the ilium, one of the bones in the toad or frog's pelvic girdle: some say it was the breast bone. Whichever bone it was, it was a *crotch* in shape; that is, a forked bone like a wish-bone, and having precisely the same shape as the frog – the horny elastic pad – in a horse's hoof.

But what is the meaning of this apparently nonsensical ritual of going to a running stream at midnight at the time of a full moon? One thing is clear to the present writer: after talking to many of the older horsemen who had performed it – men born before or about 1890 – he became convinced that they were totally involved in the ceremony. They believed implicitly in the effectiveness of their method of preparing and getting the bone, and they were certain that the bone's power stemmed as much from the special treatment it had during the ceremony as from the actual jading or drawing substances with which they after-

wards impregnated it. It was no empty show or flippant rehearsal of an ancient practice: they were in deadly earnest, serious and secret about everything concerning the frog's bone, mainly because they felt they were dealing with something that was dangerous. This is identical with the reaction of primitives to a fetich: it is animated by something they cannot understand. And as Lévy-Bruhl had pointed out,* they cannot distinguish between the fetich and the effective substances that are sometimes associated with it. If, for instance, poison were used with something, harmless in itself but merely used as a carrier, a primitive would think that the fetich is just as effective in killing as is the poison. In the same way, the old horsemen believed that the milt and the frog's or toad's bone contributed almost wholly to their skill in drawing or jading their horses. The situation for them was a total one: and it was from this totality – the ritual killing of the frog, the dismembering and the unusual behaviour of the bone in the running stream – that they gained their conviction.

The owd frog's boon

The expression the *frog's boon* was also used by the old horseman in another way that is worth recording: it was heard as a kind of metaphor for 'being in control'. If, for example, a horseman was in the field and the ploughing was going on extremely well, his stetches coming out neatly, with dead-straight furrows and a level 'top', his mate sometimes called out in recognition of his prowess:

'I see you got the owd frog's boon with you this morning.'

Belief and power

It is likely that the reader will ask at this stage: 'Is all this magical and mystical stuff worth recording!' or, as I have often been

How Natives Think, p. 67.

asked myself: 'Do you really believe in it?' But these questions miss the point. The relevant question should be: 'Did the participants, the horsemen themselves, really believe in it?' The answer is emphatically, 'Yes, they did!' It was through believing in it implicitly that they got their *power* and their results. It is no use attempting to assess this material from a purely intellectual standpoint. This is primitive material, and should be approached in the pragmatic manner of the primitives who are more concerned with the total situation than with the rational or logical aspect of it. In any experience, for instance, involving a man and a difficult horse he wishes to master, the most important element is not the animal itself but the man's mind; and especially that part of his mind over which he has no immediately willed or conscious control.

CRAFTSMEN'S WORK

The blacksmith

The smith was a key man under the old farm-horse economy; and the smithy in addition to being an essential and regular place of call was also a kind of exchange for horse and farming news in the district.

Clifford Race was born at Stonham Aspal and apprenticed to a blacksmith at Creeting. 'He was the strongest man I ever knew but he went blind through the strain of smithing. He couldn't see you if you were standing right in front of him, but he carried on at the anvil and used to feel the iron he was working.' Clifford Race volunteered for the army during the First World War and served as a farrier. When he came out he worked for some years at a stud-farm at Henley (Suffolk); then he went back to smithing and worked for many years at Needham Market, a large village near Ipswich:

'The day started at six in the morning and went on till six in the evening – even until seven at one time. The guv'nor, the mastersmith, were an old man over eighty. He were a remarkable man in his way: he went down a well to clean it out on the day he died.

I believe he were eighty-six. But in his later years he didn't come into the smithy until after breakfast. So the first man in the smithy in the morning had to pick up a hammer and strike the anvil three times – just to let the old man know we were on the job. He couldn't go off to sleep again unless he heard the anvil ring.

'The nine of us were put out to jobs like this: two were on the shoeing – two more were brought in if there was a rush; the guv'nor would be making mill-bills – a tool for trimming a millstone; two were on farm-work, sharpening the tines of harrows, mending ploughs and so on; the last four were normally on outside jobs, on pumps for wells – outside work of all kinds.

'During the twelve-hour day the two of us aimed to do thirty-six shoes, that is nine horses. Two of us averaged four shoes an hour. The town horses came in every three weeks or a month for re-shoeing. Country horses – horses that worked chiefly on the land – came in once in three months, on the average. The town horses were nearly always leg-weary, and harder to shoe. They'd lie on you as you lifted the leg: a town horse seemed double the weight of a country horse just because it were leg-weary. Another thing we noticed was this: as they were leg-weary they wore their shoes out more quickly; these town horses often did

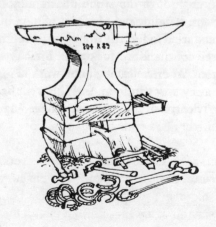

up to forty mile on the road during the day, and they got into the habit of sliding and dragging their feet. This just burned their shoes up.

'But we had one old country horse that was a bit of a nuisance – a big mare. She were a fine-looking animal, and she'd always give us trouble – but she couldn't help it, poor owd gel. She were *jink-backed*.* You couldn't back her. She had something the matter with her spine. She used to stagger, and if you didn't watch out she'd come down on you and crush you while you were a-shoeing her. When I tell you she weighed over a ton, you can see why we were a bit narvous. We used to mark her up special on the calendar; and we took care to make a right good job of her: we took an extra lot of trouble with her shoes so we could keep her away as long as we could. We'd often make the owd gel go for twenty-four weeks without coming to us. She were a beautiful bay mare with feet like butcher's blocks. You

*Or *sway-backed*: 'A horse is said to be sway'd in the back when, by too great a burthen, or by some slip, strain, or over hasty and straight turning, he hath taken an extreme wrinch in the lower part of his back below the short ribs, and directly below his fillets. . . . He will falter, and sway sometimes backwards and sometimes sidelong.' (Gervase Markham, the seventeenth-century writer on horses.)

couldn't go wrong when you were actually a-shoeing her. She had so much hoof you could bang the nails in anywhere you liked, and they'd all be right. The only thing you had to watch out was that she didn't start to stagger and put one of them feet down on you a bit sharp, or fell on you as she were a-swaying about with her jink-back.

'Jink-back is something like slipped-disc, I should say. You can tell a horse in this condition without actually trying to back him. You just want to put your hand on him and he'll start to quiver – afraid you're going to back him. It's often caused by some accident.

'There was plenty doing in the smithy when it was only horses on the farms. Sometimes there'd be eight or nine people standing about there swopping news – market news and just ordinary gossip. You hardly had room enough to do your job, but you daren't tell 'em to get out o' the way; or else they'd say they'd as much right to be there as you had! You had to go a-shoeing the horse as best you could. At election time it were well nigh impossible.

'The longest day I can remember at Needham smithy was the day of the Stowmarket Christmas sale – I forget the exact year. But up to then it had been a right mild winter. None o' the farmers had thought about having their horses *roughed*,* and they set off extra early that morning to go to the Christmas market. I cycled over from Creeting at the usual time and when I started it were all right. The roads were wet. But when I got halfway, I had to get off my bike: the roads had frozen and were like glass. By the time I got to the smithy there were a queue of horses halfway down the street, all waiting to be roughed. The farmers going to market had come down from Barking and Ringshall and those places, and on the rough owd country roads they managed; but as soon as they got to the tarred road in Needham street they had to stop. So they unharnessed the wagons, left them down the Barking road and brought the horses to the smithy.

roughing – altering a horse's shoes to enable him to walk on icy roads.

'As you know there are two kinds of *roughing*: you can either put frost-nails in the shoe or you can take it off and turn the heels and the toes of the shoes up – *turning 'em up*, we used to call it. We did a hundred and seven horses that day. We finished at ten minutes to six, about our usual time. I was just takin' off my apron in the smithy when I says to the guv'nor:

'"Was that a chain a-clinkin' in the *trav'us*?"*

'"No, there's no horses in there now!"

'"That there is! I can hear them."

'We went in and saw two of Quinton's that been sent up to be shod. We had no shoes for 'em so my mate and I had to set to and make the shoes and shoe them. It was eight o'clock when we finished. I was so tired I had to get off my bike twice on the way up to Creeting and sit on the side of the road in the snow for a spell before I could go on. That was the sort of day you don't forget. I could hardly look at my dinner when I got home. We'd worked from 6.30 a.m. until 8.00 p.m. with the shortest of breaks during the day. My mate was over seventy, so I couldn't let him lift a horse's foot after "knocking-off" time: I actually shoed the two horses. But he was laid up after that and we didn't see him for days.

traverse or partition – the screened-off portion of the smithy where horses were actually shod.

[103]

'Few people can judge what shape a particular horse is in better than the smith who shoes him. The farmers knew this; and they'd often come for advice: "Owd Todd is going to sell one of his horses – Champion, d'you know him? What sort of horse is he?" "Oh, he's all right," the verdict may be; "you can't go wrong with him." Another may come along for advice and you'd tell him to leave the horse alone: "But he looks all right! What's the matter with him?" "Maybe he looks all right; but if you buy that horse you'll be buying yourself a packet o' trouble." We lost a farm's work through something like this; only it was my boss who was involved – and it turned out all right in the end.

'The farmer's son brought a beautiful mare to be shod; and after she'd been done he asked the guv'nor what he thought on her. He studied her and in spite of her looks he told the son: "Tell your father she's a wrong 'un." When the farmer heard this judgement he was very angry, storming and swearing and saying there was nothing wrong with the mare. He refused to send his horses to be shod at our smithy after that; for once the smith's verdict got around it would be difficult for him to sell the mare. But six months later that same mare developed some complaint in her front legs. She became a cripple, and I don't know what became of her. The farmer came back to our smithy after that, bringing a couple of his horses. "You were right," he admitted, "but I was whoolly riled when I heard what you thought on her."'

Shoeing the colt

Whenever a young colt was brought to the smithy for its first shoeing few people would be found to stand around. For the colt always objected violently to having an iron shoe nailed on to its hoofs; and sometimes the smith and his assistants were thrown about the trav'us as they tried to get the young animal under control. It was no place for idle talk then: there was too much action for gossip. The danger and the extra effort needed to shoe a colt for the first time was recognized by a custom called in some districts of East Anglia by the term *First Nail* which presumably referred to the violent shock the first nail would give to the colt. Under this custom the colt's owner paid a shilling over and above the actual cost of shoeing so that the men could send out for six pints of beer as a reward for the extra effort involved.

The custom also had its echoes of other occasions. A new apprentice to the smith was treated in a symbolic way like the young colt. The men in the smithy seized him; and one of them took a hammer and drove a nail into the sole of his boot. He stopped only when the boy shouted 'Beer!', thereby agreeing to buy his new work-mates a pint each of beer. In the Brandeston forge the smith kept a four and a half gallon barrel of beer under the bench, and the men got their allowances of *First Nail* from this.

There was also a custom by which a boy at his first harvest under the old system of farming went through the ordeal of *First Nail* or *Shoeing the Colt*. As soon as he entered the first field to be cut his mates up-ended him and gave him the same treatment which stopped only when he shouted 'Beer!'.

William Gardner and Mr Flowerdew

'My grandfather moved to Billingford and he settled in and opened up the blacksmith shop . . . After a short while he found that the gypsies were taking their horses to him to be shod; and he had quite a busy time shoeing gypsy horses. He always said:

"I really owe a lot of thanks to the gypsies for helping me in my start." Anyhow, he got a few horses from Besthorpe Hall, and one or two of the little farms; and he jogged along until the time came when Mr Flowerdew* came into Diss on a market day, and he saw my grandfather. He'd come into Diss to pay a bill at Aldrich's the ironmongers. He said:

'"You haven't got time to be in Diss. You want to be home looking after your business."

'"Well," Grandfather said, "I don't get any business from you, so I don't have to thank you."

'Anyhow, Grandfather had been down to John Aldrich's at the bottom of the hill and he'd bought himself a grin'stone for sharpening tools. And he said to Aldrich:

'"Now, can I pay half this month and half the next?"

'So they said: "Who are you?"

'He told them who he was and where he'd come from, and they told him: "Come back in an hour's time and we'll see."

'He went back and they said, Yes, he could have it, and their horse and trolley was going round there at a certain date and would deliver it. So Grandfather said: "Thank you very much", and he got home. And who should walk into the blacksmith shop but this Mr Flowerdew:

'"You're a determined man to stay here, aren't you?"

'"Yes, I am; and I'm going to make it my home."

*The owner and farmer of Billingford Hall.

'"And you've been to Diss today and bought yourself a grin'stone?"

'"Yes. How did you know?"

'"Well, if it hadn't been for me, you wouldn't have had it, because they asked me your character. And I could have given you a bad one or I could have given you a good one. But I told them they didn't want to worry, I would pay for the grin'stone. So I paid for it. So," he said, "you now owe me the money."

'"Well, of all the nerve! To think they would come and ask you! But I don't want the grin'stone. They can take it back. I won't have it!"

'"Oh yes you will. You'll have it. And don't you send it back either."

'Well, my grandfather erected it; and of an evening he would be very busy sharpening up chopping hooks and one thing and another. He went on making different things – sets of harrows he used to re-lay. But he still didn't have any work from this Mr Flowerdew. Although Mr Flowerdew used to come down occasionally and see him: sometimes they would have a row and sometimes they were quite friendly. Anyhow, my grandfather he still carried on. Then one day Mr Flowerdew he went out and bought a horse, a rather special horse; and when he wanted it shod he sent it to the blacksmith shop at Scole, Mr Woodcock's.

And he couldn't shoe it. So he sent it to Hoxne: they couldn't shoe it. Thorpe Abbots: they couldn't shoe it. He went to Broome: they couldn't shoe it. So he said to the man who led the horse, Sam Burch:

'"Take it and try that man at Billingford," he said.

'So they brought the horse down, and Grandfather said:

'"Well, we won't have it in the trav'us; we'll have it outside."

'Over the trav'us door, on the top, he had a hooked ring; and he tied the horse to this ring. So he walked round it and he patted it, and he said to Sam Burch:

'"Do you like beer?"

'"Oh yes," he said, "I like beer."

'"Well," he said, "you go in the pub and have a pint of beer. You don't want to be in any hurry. I shall see what I can do with this horse."

'When Sam Burch came out of the pub he said:

'"Oh, my word!" he said, "you got two shoes on the back feet. However did you do it?"

'"Oh," he said, "that's easy, bo'," he said. "Have you drunk your beer?"

'"Yes, I've drunk my beer."

'"Well, you'd better go back and have another one."

'He sent him back to the pub; he sat there for a while, and when he came back he'd got the front shoes on. Rasped the feet all up, and blacked them with black; made them look spick and span.

'"Here you are, my man," he said. "You can take that home."

'So Sam Burch took the horse home, and Mr Flowerdew looked at it.

'"O my word!" he said, "what a tradesman! How did he do it?"

'So Sam said: "I don't know."

'"You don't know!"

'"No," he said, "if I'd ha' stopped he wouldn't have shod it. He sent me into the pub to have a drink, and when I came out he had the two back shoes on. I went back into the pub: came out and it was finished, and I brought it home."

'"You left the horse in his care?"

'"Why, yes."

'"Well, you are sacked!"

'And he sacked him on the spot. And Sam Burch went to see my grandfather next day and he said:

'"I got the sack over that horse."

'"Why?"

'"He wanted to know how you did it?"

'"Well, if you'd ha' stood here I wouldn't have done it. I should have sent it back. As you went into the pub I wanted to prove to your master I could do it. But I didn't want you to see how I done it."

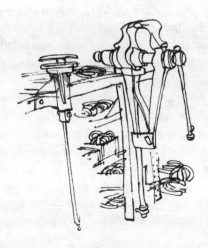

'The next time the horse came back to my grandfather to be shod. "No," he said to Mr Flowerdew. "I'm not shoeing that horse. You take your bad horses where you take your good ones."

'"Oh, that's like that is it?"

'"Yes, that is. And another thing you haven't paid me for shoeing the horse the last time."

'"Oh," he said, "you think I can't pay you?"

'"I don't think anything of the kind, but you haven't paid me."

'"Well, I'll pay you."

'"I want double for shoeing that horse because it's a bad one."

'"I'm not going to pay you double."

'"If you don't pay double I shall take those shoes off and no one else will ever put them on."

'"Well," he said, "I want you to take them off; but those shoes are so good I want you to put them back on again."

'"Would you pay me double?"

'So Mr Flowerdew he did pay him double; and my grandfather said:

'"Now take the horse away. I won't shoe it unless I have some of your good ones."

'"Now look! If I give you all the horses to shoe off Billingford Hall Farm, will you shoe this horse?"

'"Yes," my grandfather said. "You go and give that in writing to my wife in the house. She can read."

'And he tied the horse up; took the shoes off and put them back on again. Mr Flowerdew said: "That's easy. Is that all you done?"

'"Yes," and he said to Mr Flowerdew: "Now you pick hold of the hair on the heel of the horse and lift the foot up."

'Of course, Mr Flowerdew he put his hand out and took hold of the hair; and the horse nearly went berserk. And this is what the other blacksmiths had done: they'd got hold of the horse's hair and the horse couldn't bear it to be touched. Well, my grandfather he used to put the claw of his hammer under the hoof, and he picked it up. And when he'd got it up he put his hand under the hoof, laid it on his left knee and cleaned it – and that's how he shod it. He said:

'"I didn't pull or touch a hair on the horse ᴐ leg to have any effect. I knew what was wrong with that when it came to me. I've had one or two before, but perhaps not so bad."

'Anyhow, he got all the horses from Billingford Hall; and about a month later he got the horses from Hoxne farms, and some time later he got all the horses from Redgrave farms. They were all going there. From Redgrave they used to start at six in the morning; and there used to be a string of horses, tied head to tail, going from Redgrave to Billingford. And he used to do the lot in one day: it was too far to go backwards and forwards with one or two. The Hoxne farms, they always went in fours, and the Billingford farms, too, always went in fours.'

'My grandfather died in 1935 at the age of eighty-eight. But there's something I didn't tell you. Some time after he retired (he worked until he was seventy-five or seventy-six: he shod his own pony a month before he died) he said to my father:

'"Are you going to Ipswich market next Tuesday?"

'He said, Yes: he drove a horse and cart in those days.

'"Well, I'll go as far as Claydon with you, and I would like to get off and walk through a footpath into a lane and into Creeting, to have a look at the old blacksmith shop. I haven't seen it for sixty year."

'So my father took him, and he got off the cart and off he went. And when he got into this lane he was about a hundred yards off the village. There was a stile there and an old man

beside it. And Grandfather went and spoke to him, and got talking about one or two things; and my grandfather said:

'"It was sixty years ago since I left this place, I used to work for the blacksmith."

'"Well, if you worked for the blacksmith," this old man said, "that was me!"

'And the old man said that he had talked about my grandfather many times and he said:

'"I've always said you were the best blacksmith I ever had."

'"You must be over a hundred!"

'"Yes, I am; and this should call for a little celebration."

'So they went up to the village pub and had a few drinks. And grandfather caught a bus up to Ipswich market where my father was, and they drove home. He said:

'"This has been in my mind for a long, long time. I must have chosen this day to have gone and met this man. This has really made my life."'

Re-tyring cart wheels

In addition to shoeing horses and doing various repair jobs, one regular task at the smithy was the re-tyring of cart wheels. In the summer the woodwork in the farm cart or wagon wheels tended to shrink; and the iron tyres often worked loose. The wheels then needed the smith's attention.

'When this happened some farmers used to say: "I can't afford to hev the wheels done," and they'd stand the cart or the wagon in a pond until the felloes of the wheel swelled up.* The wheels would be all right for a couple of days; then they'd become ten times worse and they'd have to come to the smithy. We took off the iron tyres, and cut out a small piece off each one and then welded the ends back together. Then we fitted each tyre back on to the wheel which was clamped down on the tyring

*cf. Constable's *Haywain*. See also *Kilvert's Diary*, 29 July 1870: 'The horses were driven into a pond in order to drink and cool their heels and tighten the tyres of the omnibus wheels. (What a beautifully accidental couplet.)' Penguin edition p. 68.

platform. This was a circular steel plate, level with the ground, fixed permanently in the lane outside the *trav'us*. But first we had to heat up the tyre in the oven we'd built on purpose to do this. The oven was made of sheets of iron, in sections; and you could fit it or pin it together and dismantle it after use. It was circular in shape and we could fit it up to take any number of wheels – three or four pairs if need be. To heat the oven we placed shavings and wood in between and around the tyres which usually took about an hour to heat sufficiently. To get the tyres out of the oven two of us would have a long rod each. We'd marked every tyre, but sometimes we'd fish the wrong one out; then there'd be some swearing.

'The reason the tyres were heated was this: when we cut out the piece of the loose tyre and welded it together it was then smaller than the actual woodwork on the wheel. How much smaller we had to estimate before cutting the tyre in the first place. If it was a newish wheel and the joints between the felloes had a fair gap we'd give her perhaps ⅞ of an inch; if the joints were not very loose we'd give her perhaps ½ an inch. That meant the tyre would be that amount smaller than the actual wheel, so we had to heat up the tyre to expand it in order to get it on to the rim. Then, when the heated tyre gradually cooled, it contracted and drew the joints together and bedded itself firmly round the woodwork. There was a central spindle on the tyring platform, and the wheel was put over this and clamped down so that it wouldn't *spring*. Three men were needed to do the actual fitting of the tyre: two holding the tyre after they had taken it out of the oven, and one with a bucket of water to pour on to the felloes to stop them from taking fire as the tyre was clamped on. If it had been properly heated it would slip on without any trouble. But if the tyre had not been expanded enough, we'd have to have levers and gently lever and hammer it on, something in the same way as you'd do with a bicycle tyre. But if you hammered you had to careful to miss the joints: the felloes were dowelled together and if you hit one of the joints the wrong way, the dowel was certain to break. The owd guv'nor was a knowing one with these tyring jobs. He weren't very brisk in the morning, and often we were a bit late getting off the mark ourselves; but he didn't mind us working beyond six in the evening – we didn't get paid for that! He'd say about four: "We'll fire the oven." It would take about an hour and a half to fix and heat up the oven; and, of course, once it was started we had to carry on with the job of re-tyring. I've known him more than once take out his watch halfway through a tyring job and say as though he was some bit surprised:

'"It's six o'clock! Wheriver has the day gone!"'

But it wasn't all work at the smithy. They used to have an occasional break; and even the most unlikely incident was seized upon to make some diversion in the monotony of the work.

'After bending over a horse or a job on the anvil till all your body ached you were glad of any bit of fun for a couple o' minutes to take your mind off the job. I allus remember the owd boy from Creeting College [farm] and the fly. There was a big owd fly settled on the smithy door; and this owd boy took off his hat and was just a-goin' to swipe this fly off the door. But the guv'nor dropped his hammer and said some serious: "Don't do that! Don't kill that fly. That's our pal. That's our pal!" And the poor owd boy put his hat back on sheepish like and watched the fly zooming about the smithy, giving us a look as the same time. We often used to laugh about the owd boy and the fly.'

Some of the boys who had just left school used to be *mischieful* when they brought the farm-horses in, but the smith had a few tricks to put them in their place. 'One of the things he did was this: On the quiet he'd heat up the ends of two thin iron rods. Then he'd ask one of the boys: "Can you play the kittle-drum on the anvil like this? Sounds good don't it?" After showing the boy how it was done, he'd offer him the two iron rods – the *hot ends* towards him. The boy would drop them immediately. Then the smith said innocently:

' "Well, that's a rum 'un. I can hold 'em quite well. Or maybe, the other ends got hot while I was a-tapping them on the anvil."

' "You hold the other end and see," the boy usually said, a bit angry. But the laugh was on him, and he'd be on his way to finding his proper place in the smithy – which was to stand by and watch, and not ask too many questions.'

CLIFFORD RACE

The harness-maker

The horseman took a great pride in his horses, as we have seen; and when he turned out on the highway he was careful to see they were braided up, the brasses highly polished, and the *bounces* – the 'lovely coloured worsted', as one horseman called them – properly displayed. Many Suffolk horsemen, when occasionally they took their horses to Ipswich market, rose very early in the morning – three o'clock, or even earlier – to put the finishing touches to harness they had perhaps oiled the night before, and to paint the horses' hoofs with harness oil to make them look smart. The horseman was very particular about his harness and was as much concerned as the farmer to keep it in good order, making frequent visits to the saddler or harness-maker who had his shop in most of the larger villages.

Here is an account from one of them, Leonard Aldous of Debenham:

'I've just completed fifty-one years [1964] in the business. I left school at the early age of twelve and a half, my father having died when I was nine. We were living quite near a saddler's shop in Debenham, and I was always interested in it. The old gentleman who was the owner of the shop encouraged me and helped me along into the business. I went as an apprentice to him, starting on March 17th, 1913. My wages were sixpence per week. If I'd been fourteen years old I should have commanded one shilling, but being only twelve and a half I got sixpence.

'After I'd been at the shop roughly eighteen months – that was in August 1914 – the Great War broke out; and as two of our workmen joined the armed forces I had more or less to be pushed on. Within two years of starting my apprenticeship I was having to do roughly a man's work, but my wages were only half a crown a week.

'We used to go round the farms to collect the harness-work and bring back sets of harness for repair. But in my early days it was quite common for some of the old horsemen to walk anything up to two or three miles, and sometimes more, to bring harness down to the shop. They came down in their own time, after they'd left off work, and they'd have a small job done; and then they'd take it back ready for work the next morning. The main reason was that these horsemen were so jealous, in a way, and particular about their horses that they wouldn't put another piece of harness on belonging to another horse. Each horse had his own harness; and if it couldn't be spared to be sent down to the shop for repair, the horseman brought it himself, got it seen to and took it back ready for work on the next day.

'He made a special journey walking, as I say, perhaps three or four miles. But I should say very often the old Guv'nor would let him have either a shilling to go down to the pub while we did the job, or else he would provide him with a jug of home-brewed beer and bread and cheese. The Guv'nor used to brew his own beer in those days as most people did.'

But the harness-maker was directly involved with the farm in another way, as Leonard Aldous recalled:

'We contributed to the harvest *horkey* or *largesse-spending*, the *frolic* the men had after the harvest was gathered in. Usually the horseman on the farm – the head horseman – came round after the harvest and made a collection from the various tradesmen who'd had business with the farm – saddler, farrier, wheelwright and so on. When I was young the money the tradesmen gave

went to augment the beer-money for the frolic. The farmer probably found the food and our largesse-money was used to find the beer. Very often, too, when we were travelling round the farms doing repairs (and many of these were done just before harvest to prevent hold-ups at a busy time) the Guv'nor would tell us to leave two shillings at a certain farm, half a crown perhaps at another, and at some only a shilling: that would go towards the men's largesse-spending.'

When Leonard Aldous started in the harness-maker's shop the business was often referred to by a different name. A farmer might tell one of his workmen: 'You'd better take that *dutfin* [bridle] to the *knacker's.*' Both these words were used in medieval times; and we can understand the word *knacker* as an equivalent for harness-maker when we learn that it comes from an Icelandic root, *knakkr*, meaning a saddle. The old saddler used to prepare and tan the leather himself, and even slaughter the horses; and this last function has given the word its more usual modern meaning.

Leonard Aldous used the same tools and made the same type of harness as his predecessors did in medieval times. Some of them are described by Tusser in his *Husbandly Furniture*:

> *Whole bridle and saddle, whitleather and nall,*
> *with collar and harness for thiller and all.*

Whit- or white-leather was leather that had been dressed with alum, and it was often horse-leather. A nall is an awl (compare nadder, the original form of adder). Thiller – often *fill'us* or fill-horse in the East Anglian dialect – was a word Shakespeare used in *The Merchant of Venice*. It meant the horse that was placed between the shaft of a cart, as opposed to the trace-horse which pulled in front of the thiller.

Lining and sign-writing

'When the vehicle was finished we painted it up. Then one of the travelling craftsmen came out from the town and *lined* the cart, trap or wagon we happened to be making: that means he painted the finishing touches, the lines on the wheels and the panels. The liner did nothing else except lining and sign-writing. To line the cart he used long, narrow brushes he called *pencils*. He dipped these in the paint and lined the spokes, felloes, and sides of the vehicles as a final decoration. I well recollect one liner who used to come out here. He would walk from Ipswich and get to Witnesham soon after 6 a.m. – a five or six miles' journey. And then he'd be in a rare way because our employer was not out of bed. Like a good many other liners he enjoyed a glass of beer. In fact this one used to drink like a herren [herring]. He'd soon be shouting at the window to call the boss up to go and get him some drink – usually home-brewed beer. One of the first things he said on reaching here in the early morning was: "Is the boss up? Are his blinds up?" As soon as the boss was stirring he'd get his mug of beer; and then he'd start his lining, and not before.'

PERCY WILSON

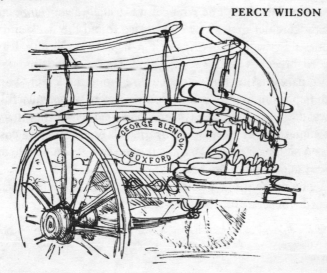

CLOTHES

The horseman's dress

For work the horseman of this period wore a sleeved waistcoat with a velvet front and *cantoon** back and sleeves. This waistcoat had flap-pockets and reached down almost to the knees: it was fastened right up to the neck with horse-shoe buttons, leaving just enough space for the red-spotted muffler or *wrapper* to be seen underneath. The wrapper was usually a very large coloured handkerchief that was wound twice round the neck and tied at one side 'with two ends left a-flapping'. On the legs were cord-breeches and *knee-buskins*. These were similar to the ordinary buskins but extended up beyond the knee: 'They used to flap about as you walked; but they were whoolly useful in bad weather.' On the feet were *home-made* boots with double tongues: 'They were made by the village cobbler and cost fourteen shillings: they'd last about two years if you got them *clumped*† at the end of the first year.'

For walking out and for Sundays he had a cord jacket and cord trousers. But the trousers were no ordinary trousers: they

canton-flannel – cotton cloth on which a nap was raised in imitation of wool.
†A *clump* is a half-sole of leather riveted on to the original sole before this wears through.

[120]

were *whole-falls*, that is, trousers with a flap that let down in front like a sailor's. They were also bell-bottomed, with a sixteen-inch knee and a twenty-two-inch bottom. The outside of the trouser-leg was trimmed with steel-faced horse-shoe buttons. Some of the more dress-conscious horsemen ordered a special kind of trimming on the leg – an inlet or gusset of black velvet, running from the bottom of the trousers, on the outside, and tapering to a point somewhere near the knee. Four or five horse-shoe buttons were sewn to this gusset as an extra decoration.

The jacket had flap-pockets; and fancy stitching on the jacket was usual. 'They'd have what we called a *vandyck* back and sleeves – a fancy stitch something like waves – on the shoulders and the cuffs. Some of them wanted pint-pots worked in fancy stitch on the back, or maybe a horse's head or even a fox-head. The owd horseman knew what he wanted; and it weren't no use a-tryin' to tell him what to have. Those owd country-bo's had wunnerful good clothes: do you know that? They went in for warmth. They'd have their breeches and leggin's lined with flannelette – lined with *swansdown*, they used to say – or fluffy calico. The cloth for their suits was *cord* (corduroy), as I've told you; but sometimes they went in for a suit of heavy tweed – *staple tweed* it was called; and at that time they made it as hard as a board. It were wunnerful stuff. It never wore up. It lasted them fourteen or fifteen years. The cost? Well, about fifty year ago a suit of staple tweed cost £3 10s. Now today ... but aside from the cost I couldn't make a suit like that today: I couldn't get the material. Breeches and leggings cost 17s. 6d.

'They dressed warm and comfortable, a style of their own. A big silver chain across the front of the weskit, and a big owd tarnip watch at the end of it. On the head they wore a hard hat with a high crown, or a billy cock with a pheasant's or wood-cock's feather tucked into the band at the side. We sometimes made an overcoat for one of those owd country-bo's – a head horseman, for instance. This was always a *melton* overcoat. Melton is a thick, very tightly woven woollen cloth. The weave is so tight, wet will never get through it. Here's a piece of real owd

melton, the owd stuff. I keep it specially to remind me what it was like. Feel it. And feel this. Here's a piece of what they make and call melton today. They still *call* it melton; but look at the difference: the heart has gone right out of the cloth. The owd stuff wouldn't wear up. You could hand the overcoat over to your son when you'd finished with it; and he could hand it over to his son.'

FRANK WHYNES

It appears that the farm-worker of [the 1900s] paid great attention to the type of corduroy he chose for his everyday clothes, and especially for his walking-out dress. There were many kinds of corduroy on the market to satisfy him. The *cords* were chiefly made by the Lancashire mills; and a firm from Peterborough – Brown and Son – distributed large quantities over East Anglia. Some of their chief varieties were: *Pheasant-Eye, Genoa, Thick Sett, Doncaster, Fine Reed, Nine Shift* and *Partridge.* Arthur Pluck has added a note about two of these:

'In the *Pheasant-Eye* cord they copied the colours of the pheasant's eye: it was a brownish cord patterned with "eyes" that stood up a bit redder. But the *Doncaster Cord* was in many ways the most interesting. It was woven to represent a field that had been horse-ploughed in the old narrow stetches. You'd have a band of ribs together to represent the furrows in a stetch; then a small gap to show the water furrows between the stetches. Often times when I was going into the country after orders and so on in the autumn, I'd look at a field that had been freshly ploughed up after the harvest; and I'd think to myself how much like a piece of *Doncaster Cord* it was – colour, straight lines and everything.'

ARTHUR PLUCK

THE HAY TRADE

Charles Hancy

'It was hard work handling the trusses.* Then you say *hard work*! Everything is hard. You can make hard work of an easy job if you don't know the right way to go. I mean in the hay trade, there was really a knack in it. You know, that's in the days when I was seventeen year old, I could go'n stick a fork into a truss weighing into eleven stone and pitch thet up high as you like with a fork, as high as I could reach. And when you couldn't reach no higher, you'd get hold of the truss and chuck it on your head, and go up the ladder like the deuce with it. That was more a knack that was – the knack o' doing on it, knowing how to get hold of it, and how to stick your fork into it. The same as when we got to Norwich and them places, we used to pitch the trusses up into the *wicket*. We used to do that with a fork – into the loft. The loft was nearly always above the stable.'

---

*A truss of hay, cut from the stack and tied compactly, of standard weight: old hay 56 lbs, new hay 60 lbs.

Evelina Goddard

'You've seen a hay-knife? Well, we had one man who could cut a truss of hay almost to a pound. You see, hay varies so. Some of it is very light and some of it is heavy. Well, then we had ... my father was very keen on stover which is really clover-hay. Well, that must *heat* a bit, and it must smell a bit. My father, passing a stack, would say:

'"That's all right! I can smell it."

'He also had a hay-iron. Have you seen one? You push it in the stack, twist it round and pull it out like that; and then smell the hay that comes out on its end. You could measure with it as well. The iron was in two parts which you could screw together. He had a little leather case to put it in, terribly fussy! I should think it measured about two yards. I've been with my father when he measured up the stack. You measured round the stack; and the thing was, some of the hay was heavy and some was light. My father gauged that by this iron; from feeling its weight; how it went into the stack. And then he had a wonderful form of arithmetic; and he divided up to see how much the stack weighed. Sometimes, you see, the farmers liked to sell the hay by the stack: "Now you buy the lot!" Others liked to sell it by the ton; measure it out after it had been trussed. Yes, at the end of the hay-iron was a hook, and some of the hay caught on that; and

he pulled it out. If it wasn't *nosey* – it must be *nosey*!, it must be scented. Well, now I've been past many a field of hay but it doesn't smell like it used to in my young days. I suppose it's all the chemicals they're putting on.

'My father turned farmer – well, small farmer: he had about two hundred acres; and my brother and I spent days in the fields. We had a thing what we called a hay-strewer; and we had an old horse that we put in this hay-strewer. My brother and I used to sit together and drive this old horse up and down the field and throw the hay all over the place to get the sun. Then probably, if the weather was fine the next day or two, we would go and drag-rake it up with another horse in a drag-rake; and then rake it all up and put it on the cock. But it must be sweet!'

The hay trade

Charles Hancy relates his experiences in travelling about on the hay business:

'When I went to school, I weren't above eight or nine year old and I used to have to go hawking milk, as I told you, before I went to school; and then I used to take the empty cans to school, bring them home at dinner-time. And as soon as I got a little older, I tell you, they'd sell a horse, and my father hopped on the bike, come over to the school and got me out; and I come home here, hopped on the old horse's back and rode to Yarmouth or Norwich, wherever they sold it. First time I went to Norwich alone, he come up to school and got me out at half past nine in the morning. I hadn't been there long. (As I told you, I had to be along with these owd horses and cows in the morning about six o'clock. Other chaps, other boys wouldn't set along o' me at school. I used to smell of the old cows. I used to get scrapping and fighting with them, with the boys at school, through thet sort of thing.) Well, the old chap come and got me out of school that morning to take this horse to Norwich. He gave me a shilling, and three pence to come home with. That's what he gave me. He gave me a shilling to give the man when I got there. The man

was going to meet me at the bottom of Ber Street. "You go straight down to Norwich down to Ber Street, the man will be a-waiting for you." That was the orders I had. Off I go; just an old sack chucked on the horse's back, no saddle or anything. My backside has been raw. I had sores on there as big as pennies. Each side of my backside raw through riding the owd horses. But I went down the bottom of this street, and the man stood there waiting for me. I gave him that shilling. He took it in the pub and he got three quarts of beer; and he had to lay a penny down and bought me a bottle of *pop*. And he stood there and he got three quarts o' beer into him. It was only tuppence a pint then. I had to come home by carrier's cart. There was a man away from Bungay – Charlie Reynolds his name was – and he took the carrier's cart for Gardiner from the bottom of Bridge Street there. He had a horse and cart and he'd go to Norwich and bring home all the parcels and that for all the tradesmen here in Bungay. And he used to deliver to little shops, little old shops, to Brooke and Woodton on the way home. I rode home along with him: he never used to charge me nothing because I used to deliver these here up to the shops for him. It cost tuppence for a ride home from Norwich.

'August 1914 when the war broke out I was thirteen year old. My father come up to school, he come up there on a bike to see the schoolmaster and get me out to get a load of hay home. Chaps had been called up into the army, nearly all of them that worked with us, they were all on army reserve. We lost five chaps in about a fortnight; and the work was left for us grandsons, the boys, to do. I happened to be just about the oldest one of the team of them really. My job was then, I had to deliver this hay. They used to get us home during the day, and when I come home from Norwich delivering a load of hay, there'd be another load waiting for me. Say, I'd get away at two o'clock in the morning. Sometimes we got to be down at Bullard's brewery by

[128]

six o'clock in the morning with a load, because they'd start loading the beer up at six o'clock; and if you weren't in the yard afore they started you couldn't get in at all. We used to take hay down to the cavalry barracks in Norwich. I've seen thirteen to fourteen load of hay stand out there, all ready for the officer to come along and inspect it. He'd inspect it and pass the load before he'd let you into the barrack ground.

'But we used to take a lot o' pride in the hay, and it was all trussed up with – good tradesmen trussed it up, you know. We'd be down there with a load and they used to come along and inspect it. We never had one – well, I can remember having one load turned away, one day. I took a load – my uncle was a-driving that: I took another load down there with him. We come along and they passed my load and they turned his load away. And he took his up on Norwich Hill; took the horses out and come home to Bungay with the horses behind me on the empty cart or trolley. And I had to go back to Norwich the next morning with a load. And I unloaded at Mr Riggs on Norwich Hill (he used to contract for all the horses with the post-office; and we used to take hay there), and I pulled the load into his yard; took the horses out, and put them into this load what my uncle – what they sent away. And I took that straight to the barracks, and they accepted it! I had a smiling face, I expect.

'Well, they inspected it; they'd go along and pull a piece out and examine it, smell it. And the best load of hay – he'd come out and ask me at the finish. He say: "Which is the best load of hay here?" Perhaps there's a dozen load of hay, and I'd walk along with him. I never used to pick out our load. There'd be Sam Smith, and Allen another hay-dealer, and I'd walk with this officer and he say:

' "Which is the best here?"

' "This is a good load of hay, sir," I say; and he say:

' "Take that load," he say, "up to the officers' quarters."

'I was nearly allus sure of getting my load in. Well, they used to say often:

' "It's a bit off, you have to come along and inspect the hay."

' "That's all right."

' "Well, take that load through."

Caring for horses

'You wanted your hosses to look better than other people's. You didn't want them to look as well: you wanted them to look better. Their owd coats and their owd manes used to shine like silk. Oh yes, you had to do them all: you got to have your hosses like that. They weren't like that owd motor-car: you come home and switch the motor off; and you don't see that until tomorrow morning. With a horse you want that tomorrow morning; and if you're going to leave it neglected you'd have it with sore shoulders; you'd have it lame or something of that sort. You had to set about it as soon as you got in: doing the legs if they were sweating. You got to wait. You couldn't go round and swill a pail of water into him. You got so used to it. You got be an hour, an hour and a half arter you were home afore you could leave them. After they'd cooled off a bit, you'd have to go and water them. If you got home and let them go, slosh water into them, you'd soon have some dead 'uns.'

CHARLES HANCY

CATTLE DROVERS

Norwich drovers and the cattle trade

During the latter part of the nineteenth century and up to the Second World War large numbers of Irish cattle were sold at Norwich market. The cattle landed at Holyhead, Birkenhead and Fishguard; and they came by rail to Norwich. The Irish cattle-dealers who shipped the cattle and followed them over employed local drovers to receive the cattle at Norwich. The drovers disposed the cattle, tended them until the sale-day, and when they were sold delivered them to the farmers who had bought them. Irish cattle were very popular at Norwich market because they were ideally suited for the coastal marshes in Norfolk and north Suffolk. They fattened up quickly and were ready for re-sale at Norwich within three months.

James Moore, born in Norwich, was one of the local cattle-drovers. He was employed by the Irishmen for the greater part of his working life:

'We'd often drive about 1,300 cattle on a Saturday morning. They'd be going in one continuous line through the streets. When we got to the market and the cattle were in their places the dealing would start. No Irishman had cattle in the auction sales.

They sold all their cattle by private arrangement. Each dealer dealt with the farmer who wanted to make a bid for some of his cattle. But even before the farmers had come up to the market someone had probably met them at the station, because each dealer had a tout – a local man. He used to go to the station and watch the farmers coming in; and if he saw a likely one or one he knew, he used to approach him and try to get him to a pub to have a drink and talk things over. Then when he'd softened him up he would take him up to the sale and introduce him to the dealer he was touting for – on commission, of course. They would then perhaps try to get him to another pub near the market – the Jolly Farmer or the Golden Ball (George Mutter of the Jolly Farmer used to lodge three or four Irishmen regularly). They'd then give the farmer plenty of Scotch and try to get him so he didn't care if he was giving £24 or £25 a head for bullocks.

'Each dealer knew well the cattle he'd brought from the Irish villages. One of them used to walk round with me up at the market pointing out his bullocks: "These four belong to the policeman; these four I bought off the publican; these belong to the baker." They used to bring some good cattle from Mullingar. Meath, Mullingar and Roscommon were the main places where the Irish cattle came from. At the end of the day the cattle market closed. At five o'clock* three Corporation attendants with a policeman would turn everyone off the market; and they had to take the cattle they hadn't sold with them. The Irishmen, if they had any cattle left, used to drive them into the street; and they'd carry on bargaining with the farmers under a street lamp; and when the police came along they'd move further on to another lamp until they'd sold all their cattle.'

*Signalled by the market bell which is still in position.

The marshmen

The coastal marshes where the cattle were fattened illustrate an economy and a way of life that are apart from, though necessarily linked with, the arable farming of the region. The cattle were either 'walked' down to the marshes direct from market or were brought to the nearest point by train: today they are transported by motor-lorries, and in recent years a rough road has been built right across the marshes to enable lorries to have direct access. But apart from this difference and the inevitable presence of the tractor on the marshes, the marsh way of life does not appear to have been greatly affected by the recent revolution in agriculture.

The Pettingill family live in a house that probably dates from the seventeenth century when Jan Piers Piers 'the master of the dykes' drained this part of the region. Mrs Pettingill, the ninety-four-year-old head of the family, told me:

'This house used to be known as the Seven-Mile House a long time ago before our family come to live here. A man named Dowson lived here in those days. It is seven mile from Yarmouth and used to be a kind of pub or lodging-house for wherry-men when the wherry traffic was the only kind on the river. There was another place farther down which is now the Bell, at St Olaves. That were the same kind o' place: they called it the Six Mile House.

'I was born Rose Mary Brooks at Belton on the 16th Novem-

ber 1876; and after I married George Edward Pettingill we lived away from the Island. Then my husband's father, George Elliott Pettingill (1833–1923) – Grandfather we used to call him – was left alone on the Island, living here by himself. He was an owd man well over eighty and he wanted to end his days on the *mashes* where he'd allus been. So me and my husband come to live here with our children. We had eight boys and two girls. My husband recollect when they used to climb up the stocks to put the owd canvas sails on the mill. The trouble there was to do that when the wind was rising. They used to put the cloth on for the winter and take it off during the summer. We've got to cross the river to get to the nearest shop which is about two miles away; and in the winter when the weather is bad we're more or less cut off. So we always have to lay in stores that will last us a month or six weeks – a sack, or perhaps two, of flour, and groceries and so on. One of the worst winters we had was at the start of the war, in 1940, when the river was frozen over for six weeks right to the end of March and there was two feet of snow. Of course, during that time we run out of flour and had to get water and groceries. Archie, my eldest boy who lived at Belton, used to bring the groceries down to the cart-shod at the other side of the river. We got the dog and give him a couple of rope ends in his mouth and he take them across the ice. And Archie tied one of the ropes to the box of groceries and we pull it across; and then we tie the other rope to the empty box and he pull it across empty ready to fill it up again. When we got the rope tied across, Ivy my daughter, she walk across the ice to see if it hold her. She was the first to go. When you stand in the middle of the river a hundred and twenty feet wide, and look each side of you, it's a rum 'un. You want a rope. Ivy was the first to go across. But we never did walk across the river before or since.'

BULLS AND BULLOCKS

Accidents

The encounter with the bull made a great impression on George Sadler who came to the rescue; and he left a written account of it. As he said, it was an episode he would never forget. He wrote it down in his ledger which he used as a kind of diary-cum-commonplace book: and by the vigour of his writing he has brought the encounter vividly to life:

'My father-in-law was a silly old man in some ways. As you have been told, he kept a herd of cows, and also a bull. This bull was a bit furious at times. He lived in a good loose-box, and was let out to water twice a day. This day, Merry – my father-in-law – had got him out; and the bull was not keen on going to drink. The water-trough was about twelve yards from the barn door where I had just appeared; and between the door and the water-trough was a single post. I could see that the old bull was not going to be forced to drink, and he protested by coming after my father-in-law who made for the post. I shouted:

' "He will knock you arse over head!"

'But Merry left that post to run into the barn near me. Now that bull weighed nearly a ton, but he leapt off the ground like a bird; hit Merry in the back and knelt down and got his horn between Merry's legs. He then tried to toss him in the air. But the bull was kneeling on Merry's overcoat; and that saved him! It ripped the coat right up. I got a two-tine fork and shoved it into the bull's neck and shouted. The bull withdrew a bit, and I said to Merry:

' "Get to that pigsty!"

'He managed to get almost there while I was fighting a rearguard and desperate battle with the bull. Merry collapsed on a heap of mud, and the bull tried his damnedest to get him. But Merry crawled and got into the pigsty; and I almost fell on top of him and slammed the door. I said to my in-law:

' "You silly old bugger! We could both have been killed!"

'But Merry had about six weeks laid up over it. A neighbour of ours heard me shouting, came and looked over the fence, and cleared off! I had a pair of slacks on, tied round the waist with a necktie (I always do this). Well, that tie broke and my trousers kept coming down; and that added to the trouble. I shall never forget that! Of course, the bull would have killed him had I not been there.'

Ploughing with bullocks

'Now when we lived at Tunstead [near Wroxham, Norfolk] they used to plough with bullocks there. I was a lad, and there was a farm not far off us. There were two chaps, two brothers, kept four bullocks; and they used to take two of these owd bullocks out – two owd long-horns – and they used to break 'em in to use 'em. That was in my time. They had collars, no yoke; put the collars on and strap 'em up top. They ploughed with 'em; and when they ploughed round the field, they'd go right steady; and if there were old roots anywhere they wouldn't break nothing. That were nice a-seeing on 'em. And I've seen a bullock and a horse a-ploughing and a-harrowing. Yeh, I see a bullock and a horse. That's true that is! And when they fed these bullocks – when they had their breakfast they used to lay down; and they'd take 'em home and put 'em out in the yard and feed 'em just the same as these other bullocks with these owd skeps. Another time I happened to look and there was a horse and a bullock there in another field a-hoeing. I tell my brother about it. But it were a funny job to break 'em in. They broke them in like a horse, but you couldn't get their necks like a horse. And they would stick their horns into the ground and into the hedge. They would! They had these big old long horns. But they used to break 'em in; and that's funny, the bullocks knew; they knew *cuppy* and *wheesh** just like a horse. They'd break them in. Some people think I'm *running on*;† but that's a long time ago. They wouldn't think I'm eighty-two. They don't think that. They think: well we don't know nawthen about that.'

SAMUEL ELLWOOD

*left and right.   †joking (Lloyd's *Encyclopaedic Dictionary*, 1895).

[137]

WINDMILLS

The miller

Most East Anglian villages had a working windmill up to the beginning of this century, and many mills continued to grind corn until recent years. Very few do this now; although there are a number of mills to be seen, occasionally even with their sails turning, their stones rarely grind corn. These mills have been preserved either by the Ministry of Works (Saxtead Green post-mill in Suffolk is an example) or by local effort as a kind of museum or nostalgic landmark in the countryside.

The miller down the ages has made his own peculiar contribution to the low esteem in which he was held. Chaucer's proto-type, the Miller of Trumpington, was such a well-trained rogue that he could distinguish between the various degrees of filching; and he could steal as occasion served him, either 'courteously' or right 'outrageously'. And Chaucer's portrait of the miller has probably done as much as the hated medieval monopoly to give the miller a black mark. Even within living memory the following saying was often quoted: 'If you find an honest miller you'll know him by the tuft of hair growing in the palm of his hand.' But to do the miller justice he could with almost equal truth reply: 'Yes, maybe. But it takes the eye of an honest man to see it.'

Mill sails

Today the mill sails are wooden vanes whose angle can be adjusted from inside the mill. But not so long ago they were actually sails and had to be put up and taken down like the sails of a ship. To enable the miller to do this more easily the arms or stocks swept to within a couple of feet of the ground. This can be seen clearly in the medieval illustrations of post-mills which originally rested on a kind of wooden tripod. The post-mill at Bourne in Cambridgeshire is a good example of the early form. Later most post-mills were supported by a round house made of bricks; and the *buck* or body of the mill raised so that the arms did not sweep as near to the ground. Although the low position of the buck was convenient in the days of the sail, it was also very dangerous. A very old – and tall – story illustrates this: a pedlar called at a mill and tied up his donkey outside. When he emerged he found that his donkey had been translated like Bottom – but up aloft.

These picturesque, turning mill sails were a delight to children; and this is borne out by Mrs Celia Jay of Blaxhall. When she was a child in the adjoining village of Tunstall, nearly eighty years ago, she and her companions used to chant the following rhyme as they watched the turning sails:

> *Father, mother, sister, brother:*
> *All go round but can't catch each other.*

MALTING AND MALTSTERS

Going to Burton

Young men who could easily find work in the East Anglian villages during the peak periods of the farming year – haysel and corn harvest – were dismissed by farmers after the harvest, and often spent the whole winter hanging about without work and without any form of subsistence except the parish or the charity of their family. These young men jumped at any chance of work during this time. Many went fishing and many went to Burton. For the malting season was complementary to the farming season: as soon as the corn harvest was over the malting began, and it went on right through the winter and early spring right up to the eve of the haysel. One stipulation the Burton firms made before taking these young workers: they wanted big-framed men, strong enough to handle the comb-sacks (sixteen stones each) of barley.

The work

'It was hard work. By gosh, it was hard work, needing good strong healthy men. I found that out myself. I mean there's chaps like myself – about twelve stone ten pounds – you were expected to carry bags of barley at sixteen stone four; and sometimes there wasn't a job for you in the hard days when there was a lot of men out of work. And there was one boss – well, if he couldn't spell your name you'd had it. You'd got to go! I remember one man called Paternoster: that's a good old Suffolk name. Yes, there wasn't a job for you if you couldn't carry the barley. It was all manhandled in those days. About eight men and a foreman had to get 300 quarters of barley off the wagons for a day's work. You had to do, that's your day's money. And the biggest – the biggest godsend that ever came to Bass's in the maltings was the endless belt. It used to carry the barley to where you wanted it instead of you having to carry it on your shoulders. I've come home once or twice with blood coming from my back-collar stud-band and my shoulder bones. You know, the skin rubbed off with carrying the barley. It was awful! I reckon it was the hardest job next to coal-mining. And coal-mining was only worse through the danger of it being underground. I've gone home at nights with clothes drenched with sweat from head to foot and the wife has had to pull my socks off, they've been that wet inside my boots. That was the heat of the kilns.'

WILL GOSLING

'The malt came off the floor and it would go into a garner, and then it all had to be screened. They did this on the screens they called *Joe and Charlie* – two big screens. You'd get your good barley and the muck would go behind the screens. You had to throw the malted barley up against the screen. It was done by a fan as well. It was hot: it would nearly kill you. We had to have masks for this. When it had been screened you'd got to be in there and the malted barley would come out of a big hole just big enough to get a comb-sack through; and it used to run into a big

[141]

heap; and you'd got to be inside there a-throwing on it back so it didn't bung up the hole. When you come out of there you was drunk from the dust of the malt – without having nawthen to drink! No, you didn't want anything to drink. You was drunk. When you come out of this you was absolutely drunk! Then if you'd lie down for a few minutes, have a few minutes' sleep, you were right again.

'For the work we used to do up there we used to have all the beer we could drink. There used to be a chap told off every day to fetch us beer in two nine-quart cans. I often had eight or nine pints before breakfast; and breakfast was at eight o'clock, when we used to get to work at two o'clock in the morning. You never got drunk from that: you were used to it and you always had it. Sweated it out turning the barley and turning the malt. But it was all rush and go: one to beat the other. Of course that was three storey high: a floor here, then the next floor, then the top floor. Three floors in a malt-house. One floor would be up against another.'

JAMES KNIGHTS

This competition between the men working on different floors was confirmed by many of the maltsters. The men on one floor would complain, for instance, that they had a thicker *piece* of barley to turn than the men on the floor above them: 'The top floor is not spreed [spread] as thick as this 'un', and so on. It was harder, therefore, to turn, and since they were on piece-work they were afraid it would affect their wage.

In the close season after the malting finished, the buildings were cleaned down thoroughly. One of the essential jobs was to clean the perforated kiln-bricks or tiles. I first heard about this job from Mrs Gwendoline Hancock of Ipswich. She used to go kiln-pricking in the maltings at Manningtree, Essex. For this she used a bent knitting needle with a cork to protect her hand. Tom Wood of Burton described the process: 'During the school holidays we used to go *kill-pricking*. We used to prick out the holes in the malting tiles. They'd get fouled up with barley and dust during the malting season. Through these holes the hot air rose from the *kill* underneath and roasted the barley, so they had to be clear. When we were kill-pricking we used to put a sack down on the floor and lie on our bellies using a bodkin to clear holes. We used to work down a row of bricks or tiles. We got a penny for each brick, and it was a wonderful thing for us to earn some money during the school holidays. We also used to catch greenfinches that came on to the barley. We caught them with a net and we used to sell them as cage-birds.'

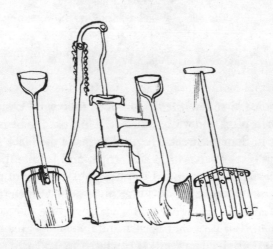

Lodging in Burton

The East Anglians were called *Norkies*, *Suffolk Punches* or *Suffolk Jims* and appear, on the whole, to have got on well with the Burtonians though there was the inevitable fracas occasionally. James Knights told me that he and his mate were once in a fight with two Burton men, and his mate – a Halesworth man – died in his lodgings two days later. The trouble usually started in a pub and Sam Friend recalled how the East Anglians would recognize some of the signs. If a Burton man turned his empty beer-pot upside down on the table they knew there was going to be trouble. So they could either stay or disengage, as it suited them. The East Anglians stood out from the local people, both by reason of their speech and their dress. Mrs Wightman remembered:

'When I first saw them I thought they were costermongers with their black and white trousers. They used to be made at Mr King's in Station Street. He used to make the black and whites and the black coats with a silk stripe; and I quite thought they were costermongers until I went to help a friend of mine – she kept a public house – and I met quite a lot of them there. So I found out who they were and what they were. They were very nice men. But we could hardly understand them sometimes in their Suffolk talk, you know. They talked peculiar.'

A barley romp

When the young East Anglian maltsters were not working they played hard, often violently. This was an understandable reaction to the gruelling nature of the work. There was also a certain amount of natural fun and horseplay in the maltings themselves when the foreman or piece-walker was out of sight.

Albert Ablett recalled the occasion over sixty years ago when a girl very rashly walked on to the malting floor when the piece-walker was not about:

'We got a young lady in there once. She'd come there, I don't know how. But she was a funny one I expect. I mean she got into this barley with us; and there was some playing about. Two or three of us, we pulled her down into the barley and pulled her drawers down and filled 'em with barley. Of course we didn't interfere with her, just pulled down her drawers, you know, and put the barley in and let her go.'

Burton teapots

The buying of a teapot was part of the Burton ritual that helped to give variety to the East Anglian's stay in the Midlands. These large, rather crudely decorated, earthenware teapots were made at Coalville and Swadlincote, and many of the East Anglians who went up before the 1914–18 war brought 'Burton teapots' back with them because it was part of the experience of going to Burton, like buying a new suit. Many of the teapots – which are identical with the old bargee's teapot – have since become family heirlooms in East Anglia; Sam Friend still has the one he brought back with him in 1912.

Braided belts

Another article the young men brought home with them was a belt. Most of them were young horsemen on the East Anglian farms and a braided belt was almost part of the dress. Most of these belts came from a nearby village of Winshill. Albert Love remembers that the young workers who went to Burton used to bring back braided leather belts from Burton for their friends. They cost half a crown each before the First World War. 'All the

young Norfolk horseman used to wear them. It was the practice to walk out of a Sunday with the braided leather belt showing just below your waistcoat. A mate brought me one down from Burton well over sixty years ago – and here you see I still got it. It was in 1902, it was; a man named Plumb got it for me. You see the fastening on the belt are all made like the horse-gear: the buckles are stirrups, and the clasp a snaffle-bit with a horse-shoe in the centre. But I found out the way to braid leather myself. I once went to a saddler in Bungay who sold these belts ready made up. I offered to braid them for him; and he paid me five shillings for half a dozen I did for him.'

THE FIRST WORLD WAR

Joining up

Almost as soon as war broke out in 1914 James Seely joined the army. He served through the war with the Eighth Norfolks, gaining the rank of sergeant and also the Military Medal:

'I first went to Shorncliffe in Kent; then Colchester, Salisbury Plain; and then France. I got to France on the 15th May 1915 and I stayed there until the 21st February 1919. We had a proper training at the beginning of the war, but I remember later drafts coming out to us – young lads from the Lancashire cotton mills, for instance. They joined the army, had *leaf*, were sent to France and were killed – all in eight weeks. Young kids! Passchendaele was the worst because of the mud and the water. You couldn't make trenches because if you dug down more than a foot or so it would fill up straight away with water. We had to make a hollow in the mud, and we lay there like swallows*: we used to long for the dark so we could stand up and straighten our legs.

*This was printed [in *Where Beards Wag All*] and a short time afterwards I had a letter from an old East Anglian farmer who asked why I had not included a note explaining 'the very ancient piece of non-knowledge' in the above. He was referring to the old belief about swallows: that they winter in the mud of rivers and streams and do not in fact migrate.

'But do you know, I think the happiest time I ever had was in the army; though there were some funny times, real bad times. But I think I can say I had some of my happiest times in the army. When we'd be overtopped with mud and water in the trench there'd allus be someone say something to make you laugh. You allus had a laugh, even if you'd been a-cryin' two minutes afore that. Somebody were sure to say or do suthen so you could have a good laugh. We were once in a dug-out, I recollect: there were only owd bits o' wood on the top of it. And it were a-raining and a-raining! You were up to and over your knees in water in the trench: it was supposed to be *our* dug-out and it was coming through these bits o' wood and we were a-sodden wet through and cold. And there was a chap there – he was a sort of chapel preacher – and he says: "Oh," he say, "I've had enough on it!", he say, "I've a good mind to shoot myself," he say, "with this lot. I can't stick it much longer."

'"Out!" said one of the blokes. "Out! Don't shoot yourself in our 'front room'. Get out and do it!"'

James Seely's experiences while he was in the army may appear out of place in the context of this book. I include them because his statement that his days on the Western Front – in spite of the horror and the squalor – were the happiest of his life seems to be some sort of commentary on the greater part of a lifetime spent in what is often regarded as the idyllic English countryside. It may have been idyllic to some but evidently not to the people who lived as close to the land as James Seely did.

A zeppelin raid

'In the First War they had – just on the Hards here – they had lines of horses there. They had a camp there and all; that's where they had all them bombs when the cows got killed. I don't know whether it was 1915 or 1916. I helped poor old Jack Wards, the horse-slaughterer. We was there all one Sunday with a trace-horse, pulling him up the common with his slaughter-cart: dead cows and that. There was a butcher here in Bungay, his name was Rodwell; he got – he was killing one of these cattle and got some of the blood in his finger or something. He had this here anthrax: it nearly killed him. He was very bad! He was killing these cattle that were wounded. It was a zeppelin raid. I can remember that as plain as anything, coming over there. There was a camp at the bottom of the common. He missed that, and caught all these cows. He missed them by about two hundred yards. He dropped seven bombs on the common there: of course, it was a boggy old place; it left a hole there you could put a house in, nearly. Yes, an old man down there in the lane, poor owd Vesey – he had a wooden leg and one eye – he kept cows: he lost two of his cows, got killed like that.

'I helped Jack Wards the horse-slaughterer on that Sunday: the old man gave me a quid, a gold sovereign at that. He gave me a sovereign. He'd put a couple of cattle on this owd cart; and I was a-pulling on 'em up, helping his horse, a-tracing on him. Yes, they called these sovereigns in. They were very scarce then. I know the last one I had I paid a doctor's bill. Dr Burstead – when I gave it to him he put it in his mouth and bit it to see that it was a good 'un. That was a doctor's bill. They were getting very scarce about 1921–1922, when I went to Burstead's. I was married then; and it was a doctor's bill for a boy – for a boy I lost.'

CHARLES HANCY

[150]

LAND AND SEA

The littoral

A region such as East Anglia illustrates the kind of terrain in which an oral historian may profitably range. The history linked with the sea has been, and is being, well documented; and the land has been exhaustively covered by the historians; but the *littoral* – the borderline area where the land is interwoven with the sea, not merely in the physical sense but chiefly in its folk-life or human connotation – has not been much studied. In this area there was also a great amount of seasonal labour-migration: farm-workers going to sea after the harvest for the home fishing – *half-breed fishermen* they used to call them in the *Saints* district of north Suffolk; and the *fishing-chaps* who bought or hired a horse or donkey and trap to hawk fish round the villages during the herring season; and there was an associated dealing in horses from Scotland to satisfy the seasonal demand. Again, the staithes or private quays in the estuaries of many East Anglian villages were used to send hay or grain direct from the farm to London or the North in barges which brought back town-manure from London or coal from the North.

James Chaplin's memories

James Chaplin was born in 1886, and during his early years at sea most of the craft were still under sail. Like many East Anglians who took to the sea he first served on the farm:

'When I first left school I stopped near Ipswich and worked there. I left: got fed up with it, I suppose. I wanted to be a roamer. So I went to Yorkshire, on the farm. That was when I was about fourteen and a half. Well, I stuck it for two years. The money there the first year was £6 a year; the next was £8; and the third year when I come away it was £12. I come home here then to Ipswich: I'd enough of Yorkshire. I worked in a dairy for about three months. He wanted you to sell more milk than the cows gave! I had to go round with a can of milk! I dunno, I thought, I'll get out of this. So I went to sea.

'I shipped in an owd ketch, an iron thing built at Falmouth; went to Plymouth with manure. We were seven to eight days from Deal to Plymouth. And I wished then I'd been on the farm, I might tell you! The wind blew seven days. But when we got there it was all right. I was going home now, I reckoned. I'd finished! But I didn't; I stuck it. We had to put a bloke in hospital there; and so the owd skipper say to me: "Boy," he says, "we ought to have another hand. But you can manage with the cooking; and the other part help your mates." I said: "All right, sir." That made us four hands. When we got to sea it was different. I thought: "I wish I'd ha' went instead of me telling him I'd stop with four hands." Anyway, we got to Saundersfoot [South Wales] for coal back to Ipswich. Well, we got back to Ipswich all right. Didn't think nothing about leaving then; got 'climatized, I suppose.

'Anyhow, we went to London from Ipswich and loaded cement for Kilrush in the Shannon in Ireland. Oh, we was there – I expect for a month. Couldn't find the skipper for a month. He was on the booze somewhere. Anyhow, we loaded kelp for Glasgow. When we got there he got a letter to say the owner had fixed up for coal for Poole in Dorset. He finished when he come there. He writ and told them he'd finished; then we all finished. We weren't going to stop there with a fresh skipper. And after that we shipped – me and another feller, an Irish feller, a Belfast man – we shipped in an owd schooner called the *Mount Blairie*: it was an old thing that had been ashore at – in a little shipyard; and they'd done her up during the winter to give them men a job. Well, I was in her for thirteen months.

'And that's how it kept going on. Ship to ship, at that time o' day; never stopped nowhere long. (That thirteen months was a long while.) Anyhow, if I was to tell you all the ships I was in, you'd want a sheet o' paper as long as this house.'

Chained boats

'Ipswich docks have changed since I first knew them over sixty years ago. They just closed the last pub down there [c. 1966]. I don't know how many there were then. The Dolphin was the well-known pub in Ipswich. It was not a very big pub: it was alongside Paul's warehouses. That's where the Norwegians and

Swedes – well, sometimes the British sailors got in – but mostly foreigners used to go. They used to come there with timber that time o' day; owd Norwegians. Some of them had chains round their boats, fore and aft, to hold them together, do they'd ha' sunk; busted right open from the swelling of the wood with too much water. Water used to come over the top, and swelled it up and bust em! They used to have big chains right round, fore and aft to keep them togither. I know, at one time o' day in Shoreham I was doing ballast – in the *Mount Blairie* that was – and the owd mate was tipping these baskets of shingle into the hold, the empty hold. And there was a Norwegian came alongside him. It was a barque with chains round it. The owd mate of the barque looked over, he say to our mate:

'"It wouldn't do to drop them baskets of shingle down in our hold!" he say. "Down we'd go! That's why we got these chains round: to hold her togither!"'

JAMES CHAPLIN

Shanties

'It was hard work but you used to have some enjoyment out of yourself. There's no enjoyment now much, is there! Wherever the pub is, whether it's in the docks or the full of the town, that doesn't make much difference. They used to sing the shanties on those big owd deep-water ships. We never used to. We never had enough of us; want all hands almost to keep even on the small ships. There weren't no shanties. Ain't got the time for shanties. We never done much singing aboard; especially on some on 'em. We didn't have enough bloody grub to sing on! That's right, with some on 'em; I'm telling yer!'

JAMES CHAPLIN

Seven and six a day

'When we loaded the lighters we got seven and six a day, at the latter end. We used to ship on Ipswich; go down – perhaps the ship'd only be there two days – come home again. If that Custom House clock was before twelve o'clock you was finished: you didn't get the next day's pay. That's how tight it was at that time o' day! That wasn't a very big screw [wage], was it? The time you done three days you was paid off. And you'd get about one day's pay of groceries and meat and stuff. So you never had a lot to come home with. It was all right if you went away to Lynn or anything like that – so that you got a week or two in. But going down to *The Bay** weren't no good for us. It might have been good for the *dockies*, but it weren't no good for the lighterman. Seven and six for a twenty-four hour day. You had no redress. *Work hard when and where you were required*: that's what was in the articles. Well, you can't get away from that, can you?'

JAMES CHAPLIN

A Jonah

'They lost a boat down here: Paul's the *Oarsman*. Well, I can't say it wasn't trimmed; but there! you never know, do you? That was loaded at Rotterdam. A strong easterly wind when she comes out; she'll do a good bit o' rolling there, jumping about with the easterly wind, anywhere in the North Sea. It's the worst wind you can get: the nor-easter, the east and the south-east. Of course, you can't say! The thing went. She was *Jonah* I expect. ... A Jonah! People who go to sea and dislike a thing they come out with it: *I say she was a Jonah*. Well, the whale swallowed Jonah, and she swallowed them; and they all went down, the whole lot of 'em, poor fellers!'

JAMES CHAPLIN

*Butterman's Bay in the River Orwell.

THE HERRING INDUSTRY

The herring girls

'The Scotch lassies came down to do the herring for the barrel processing, the same as the Dutch, the pickle processing, and some splitting for kippers in the fish-houses. To do this processing they stood out in the open, a lot of them gyping or gutting the herring. The herring then went into the barrels, then salted, and the barrels were laid in rows. A dry pickle that would turn moist. All they had to do was to take the bung out of the barrel, top off the level until they were ready to move them. These girls came down in special trains: it wasn't just the odd few. There were specials from Scotland to bring them. So it shows you the number of girls. All the end of the parade, the pleasure beach, was all what we called the *pickling plots*, where various firms had their troughs, and the girls worked. It didn't matter what the weather was like. There was no cover! They came down in September. They did their shopping, ordered their goods, and put down a deposit on them until Christmas, and then there'd be a grand climax when they all went home. Scotsmen used to buy their homes here, furniture and everything. The boats that used to go back to Scotland were all laden: pianos, bedsteads, anything they could get. You have to remember that some of them came from remote parts of Scotland, and the stores catered for them. And lots of Scotsmen used to send boxes home every week for the children – fruit, sweets. I know Yarmouth shop-keepers did a really good trade with Scotch people, just sending boxes home. Furniture would go by boats. They were only ashore, the fishermen, on a Saturday night, unless the weather was against them.

'The Scotch girls stayed in certain houses down the south end of the town. With these oilskins and boots they'd just come home and drop them outside the door and go indoors. They were always clean; but they had to dress like that. Don't get the wrong impression. Look what they had to do! Fancy standing back to the North Sea for ten hours or more handling cold fish! There was really no limit to the day: they had to work till the fish were finished. If the fish kept coming in they kept going. There was no official hours. It was incredible! They were strong, healthy and cheerful; and a match for any of their menfolk; and always knitting when not at work. Walking, talking, but always knitting! I don't know if they still breed 'em like that today.'

HERBERT SCARLES

Herring at night

'The night-scene when they were landing the herring is one never to be forgotten, especially in the early times. The whole place would be alight with flares, the old cotton flares with *waste*.

Flares on carts and boats, horses stamping, men shouting, loose herrings flying all over the place and quickly snatched up by children and men. There were no hours of work. The boats came in and were unloaded; and the fish was carted away. They worked until they were finished. It was one pandemonium. They swung the baskets, the maunds, on to the boat; they were loaded and swung ashore. As they came ashore herrings fell off, one after another. There were kids scrambling, poor men and women, all after a string full of herrings to take home. It was just hell! A few dozen herring here or there; nobody troubled: every child went home with a few dozen herring on a string. It was accepted. No one thought very much about it. It's true there was a policeman chasing the kids with a cane. But they didn't really bother. What were a few herring? You could walk from there till your feet ached, and still you'd see nothing but herring. Herring, herring! until you were sick to death of them. And of course, all the fish-houses – all the fires were going; and the whole town would smell of oak fires whichever way you turned.'

HERBERT SCARLES

Fishing from Lowestoft

'Are you interested in the actual fishing that used to go on from Lowestoft? There used to be five men go on a boat. They were little sailing boats, and they went all round, down to Ireland and Cornwall at different times. And at that time o' day they didn't get any wages. If they earned anything, when they came back to Lowestoft they had it. If they were in debt, which they were very often, they hadn't a penny. And there was this parish here, Wenhaston, and Westleton which is the next one, there were about a hundred and fifty men went to sea out of these two parishes. I've heard them say if the owners gave them their fare home from Lowestoft to Darsham, that's all they had. And the wives had been living on credit to the grocer in the village. There was one here and there was one there; and they'd stand the food until they come back. If they had a voyage they paid for it. If they didn't – well, the grocer didn't do too good. One here – they said he went bankrupt through it. But what happened at Westleton I don't know. My father was born at Westleton. I've heard him say how he went to sea and he done two voyages. He'd got married just before he went to sea, and he had two voyages and he didn't earn anything. And he was going again, but when he wanted his clothes to go my mother had cut them up and burnt them! So he had to go and get a job on the land, for ten shillings a week. I don't know how many of us were born then – three or four, I expect. (We were nine children in all: six boys and three girls.) But he had to keep us on that. But eventually he got a horse and cart, and he went into the fish trade. You didn't want above £5 or £6 to buy a horse and cart at that time o' day because it was quite a lot of money. He got into the fish trade; got on a bit and on a bit, and that's how he started going to Lowestoft and buying his own. And then he'd buy a bit so that he could send a bit to the London market – not in a very big way but enough to utilize all the money he had to do what he was doing. And you could only go as far as the money would go, couldn't you?

'And these fellers used to go to sea like that; and in these boats they were gone ten and twelve weeks, and they slept in little bunks, and they never changed their clothes the whole time. I know that! I went once. I had to go for consumption. It cured me! One week, that's all I was there. They were afraid to take me any more. There was something the doctor couldn't move on my chest – what he thought was consumption. Didn't it move! It nearly took me off. I bled on the afterdeck so much I heard the skipper say to the mate:

'"I shan't bring him any more when we get to Lowestoft." I heard him and I thought to myself:

' "I'm the best judge about that. You let me just put my foot on that shore, you'll never get me here again!"

'I never went any more. It cured me! Consumption I had, I'm told. That was my only sea-faring experience. And when I came ashore – I'd been there a week – he gave me ten bob. It was kill or cure! Did I bleed! The afterdeck – of course those boats weren't so big as they are now – all where I laid, it was all over the deck. It frightened the life out of them. But I was then – well, I didn't care if I did die. Do you know, there are some times when you feel: I can't stand this. It would be better to be dead. Yes, I went on that voyage as cook, and the beauty of it was the boat was called the *Happy Days*! But that cured me. After that I never had any illness. The only illness I ever had was twenty-five weeks in a hospital in Rouen with dysentery. (I was four and a half years on the Western Front as a stretcher bearer) and only one of the worst cases who had it and lived through it. I weighed eleven stone when I was in the Line: before I came out with that I weighed five stone ten. Then I came home to England on a stretcher. Apart from that I've never had a day's illness in my life; never been in bed a whole day. I might have been in bed with measles when I went to school, but nothing else.'

ROBERT THOMAS SPINDLER

Fish-curing

Many of the fish-trading families along this coast had their own fish-curing houses in addition to their retail business. The Spindlers were no exception.

'Fish-curing was hard work: we had a rough time. I've seen my mother standing, what they call *speeting* herren, that is putting them on sticks to make bloaters, and when she finished she had to lay down. And they'd pull her dress off her, and it was frozen stiff. I had to cart water for her. They were hard days. There were no easy days, those days. We cured all our bloaters and our kippers, at one time. Of course, they've got out of all recognition today, but three a penny fresh herren were at that time. We had two big smoke-houses in the garden. We could put ten thousand fish in one. We used to put these herren up for red-herren during the winter, and we'd probably put three lots or consignments. But we always put one particular herren what we called the *October blue-nosed* herren because they never wasted when they were hung up to be smoked. They came down almost as big as when they went up. And they used to be like ham. They used to be sent to London and various places; and when we'd done all that we got four shillings a hundred for them. And in that one house we used to do thirty thousand or more – we'll call it thirty thousand – in three hangings.

'The herren all came in barrels. My father used to go and buy them at Lowestoft. We used to curse them when we see 'em coming: we knew what we had to do: to get in and go to work. But he used to buy them and send them down home by train, and we used to cart them by horse and cart from the station.

'When you had them fresh you had a concrete floor. You threw some salt on; you pitched your herren on. Then you turned them over for twelve hours to the right, and twelve hours to the left, and up they go! Twenty-four hours' salt, and then hanging them. We burned oak, seasoned oak, and sawdust. Nothing else: it was fatal to use any bit of wood. If you used pine you'd taste it in the herren. Perhaps the oak would lay there for three or four years before we used it. We'd always get so much and we used it in rotation. The sawdust we used to get from the Peasenhall works, Smyth's the Suffolk drill-makers.'

Sam James's laziness

'There was an old man – his wife used to take in washing (laundry they call it now); and he used to bring the washing home to his wife and take it out again. He was a lazy drunkard, and they used to pay him but he never took hardly any money home. He had a donkey and cart, and the old donkey used to bring him home. He was asleep but he'd just take him home. He was only out of Yoxford a little way, and a friend of mine and myself we saw him coming – Sam James was his name. He was coming up the road, and I said to my friend:

' "I'll tell you what we'll do: we'll have a game!"

' "What are you going to do, Bob?"

'We pulled the donkey up: we took it out of the shafts, and took the shafts through the top of a five-bar gate. Then we harnessed the donkey back into the cart, head into the shafts first. So when he woke up the donkey was looking at him. Of course, it frightened the life out of him. He never drunk no more. The people in Yoxford said he never did drink no more!'

ROBERT THOMAS SPINDLER

On board a Lowestoft boat

'You had little social life on board. You had to go ashore for that. When you went ashore it would be to some pub. I remember going to Shields. There you'd get a nice night along with some of the miners. They'd tell you they wouldn't do your job, and you'd tell them you wouldn't do theirs! There was very little social life on board, but when you come home to Lowestoft, they'd go to the Suffolk, and treat one another, or to the Stone Jug, a little farther up the road. Gurdy used to have that, a teetotal fellow, a very good owd fellow. If it was getting too much, he'd stop his tap – which was a good thing – and tell 'em to get home.

'But it was good food on board, on the whole; and you could always help yourself with biscuits and a bit of cheese or something. You always had herren for breakfast. Sometimes you had to help the boy clean the fish for breakfast. And you'd get a bucket with about a hundred in. It was recognized: ten fish to each fellow. Mind you, you certainly got hungry there! The food was good, but you got fish for breakfast. You had to clean these fish out, and put about eight *snotches* in each one – bring a knife down the side of the herren, and make cuts about three-quarters of an inch apart. And when you picked hold of the fish and got hold of a piece it would come clean away. The boy cooked 'em, fried 'em. That was the boy's job, not a very pleasant one too because he had to – one of the hardest jobs I reckon, and the least paid – he had to cook the food and coil the big rope which was a nasty job, especially in the summer when the jelly-fish were about; they used to sting the hands and he'd get a rash between his fingers.'

HORACE WHITE

[163]

LANGUAGE

Sloe-hatching time

The phrase *a sloe-wind*, meaning a cold wind, gives the clue to an old belief which is mentioned every year in this village. The belief is enshrined in the proverb: '*Sloe-hatching* time is the coldest time in the year.' This is the time when the blackthorn breaks in its spectacular blossom; and, strangely enough, within the writer's experience, this period often coincides with a cold spell distinguished by east or north-east winds. It is likely, however, that the coming together of the cold and the blackthorn blossom is one of accident; and it is probable that the belief is another vestige of the primitive form of reasoning displayed in homoeopathic or imitative magic. Like produces like: the blackthorn in spring simulates the depths of winter – a blackthorn hedge in full bloom does, in fact, look as if it is covered with snow or a thick hoar-frost – therefore according to the old principle cold weather is an inevitable and logical consequence.

The countryman takes a great interest in the weather: he has to because his living is bound up with it; and he observes it as closely as a scientist watching a long and intricate experiment. The hypotheses, formed after his observations, are many; but most of them are related to the empirical findings of a long tradition and the world is spared a too individualistic interpretation of some of Nature's more self-willed manifestations.

Field names

Old dialect words are often crystallized in field names: one field here is called the *Scuts*. This word is a variant of the word *scoot*, the triangle left within the headlands after a field has been ploughed – a field, that is, of an awkward shape. Robert Savage referred to it as a *box-iron* piece, a piece of land roughly the shape of an old fashioned box-iron used for smoothing linen; and he related that the old ploughmen used to refer to the ploughing of this type of field as *goring work*. A *gore* or *gusset* is, in fact, another name for a scoot.

Another field is called *Houndses* or *Hounces*. This too, is a dialect word, seldom used now: it refers to the yellow and red worsted ornament spread over the collars of horses in a team. It occurs sometimes in old farm catalogues – a fruitful source of

old dialect words – notably in one made at Grove Farm during the last century; one item here was listed as *Hounces and Trappers*. The trappers or trappings were the breeching of the cart-harness. There are two *pightles* in this parish, both referring to elongated pieces of land, relics of the time when such shapes were left at the edge of a field after it had been divided up for strip-cultivation. There are also two *Backhouse* fields, both placed where one would expect them – overlooked by the domestic quarters of a farmhouse.

Old words and sayings

The sayings of country people, sometimes tinged with poetry, always rich in concrete images and braced with the vigour and rhythm that gives them long life, are worth revealing. The ones quoted below can be imagined against the background of village life.

When I began collecting material, one of the Blaxhall people offered me an open invitation: 'Drop in at any time if you want to know anything. If I haven't got the time I'll make time. Made time is the best time, so they tell me.'

'It snew a masterpiece.' – a young boy describing a heavy snowfall.

'Ringers and singers are no home-bringers.'

'It would sometimes be ten o'clock before I came home at night.

I'd have to dig a quarter of an acre. And it was uphill work coming home afterwards; and if I'd ha' hit a cobweb I'd ha' fallen back'uds. I was like a dead lamb's tail.'

'It was a great loss. He was a wunnerful horse, the apple of the owd boy's eye. He was a horse like in an oil-painting, with his crest like a rainbow.'

'It were a whoolly fierce wind. It took nine tailors to hold the needle up.'

'I was so mad you could boil a kittle on my hid.'

'A nice owd boy. But he's going hoom fast. I didn't know him when he got on the bus. I'd not seen him for six months. Another couple of clean shirts and he'll be gone.' – a bus conductor's comment on an old man.

'That is a real jubilant job.' – a job well done.

'He'll dig a hole for anyone.' – of a captious man.

An old gypsy woman wanted to tell Nellie, a Suffolk woman, her fortune.
    But Nellie said she 'knowed it already: she were married'.

The highest testimonial in an East Anglian village:
    'A very nice man is Mr P., quiet and never interferes with anybody.'

On old age:
    'He's the old man now. He's got no ink left in his pen.'
Or:
    'His arches have dropped. He's spent all the pennies in his purse.'

'You ought to have a pain in your tongue not your leg, then you might not use it so much.'

'She allus had pork in the pot and beer in the cask. And at harvest she'd be out raking corn behind the wagon till ten o'clock at night.'

'If you can't do what you would, do what you can.'

'Striplins! We were not very wide across the shoulder at that time of day.'

'That bike had a twenty-eight-inch frame. It was much too mighty for me.'

'The black ox has trodden on his foot.' – he has met with misfortune.

'He was put in with the bread and took out with the cakes.' – a brick-oven image: a bit underdone or, 'not quite twenty carats'.

'He has gone into the mole country.'

'They used to take an interest in the way they made corn-stacks in the old days. To make it harder for vermin to get into 'em they used to draw a wagon alongside a stack, and stand on the wagon with a scythe and then trim the stack. They moved it round the stack. Those stacks looked as if they had been turned out of a tin.'

'I was a bit staggery. But I'm a king to what I was.'

'He's such a fornicator! He tells you one thing to your face and another behind your back.'

Will–gill (or he–she) – an alternative name for a *morphadate* (hermaphrodite), a cart or vehicle which is an amalgam of a wagon and a tumbril.

Horseman: 'Artheritus it is, I reckon.'

Doctor (after examining the foot): 'Don't worry. It will get better when the cuckoo comes back.'

Horseman: 'The cuckoo! The cuckoo ha' now flown back hoom! What am I a-going to do till the lil owd basket come back agin?'

Connie Winn, an old inhabitant, was once in the dining-room of her home and there was a terrible noise coming up from the kitchen: saucepans appeared to be clattering unduly and there was an occasional crash of broken crockery:

'I made to go down the stairs to see what was happening. When I got halfway I heard the angry voice of the French maid saying very aggressively: "You got nobody like Napoleon!"

Then came the calm, decided voice of the Suffolk cook: "And don't want! We got Oliver Cromwell and all sorts."'

Michael Riviere recounts a family memory about a specific occasion in the great Paston Barn at the time of John Paston Mack. He recalls a Paston man who rode in the Charge of the Light Brigade at Balaclava:

'He came safe home and was given a celebratory dinner in the Barn. Towards the end, and no doubt full of beef and beer, they got him on to his feet; but despite encouraging shouts he was speechless. My great-grandfather, trying to help, said:

"Come on Jack! When the Charge sounded and you all began to ride forward, what was the first thing you did?"

'He came round a bit and said firmly: "I hulled away my swad."

'There was rather a stunned silence while everyone wondered why, so old John Mack said: "Hurled away your sword! What did you do that for?"

"So I could have both hands to hold on with."

'Roars of sympathetic laughter from his Paston friends. And that was all he would say. I think he wasn't much of a horseman, perhaps hadn't been in the regiment very long; and the great achievement in his eyes was that he had managed to do that long and difficult gallop without falling off. Unless he rode over one, he certainly did no harm to the Russians.'

'There he was a-sitting there like a scaly old bull.'

'The lil ol boy turned up a bit quick: he come jus in time to hev a slice of his mother's wedding cake.'

'He said he would buy me a hat and I told him we'd wait until they got the new 'uns in; but when we come to it a week or two later he wouldn't spend his money. It was my fault! I should hev let him while he had the maggot in him.'

'A young girl in her fair prime and pollen.'

'She were a big stroppolin' *mawther* [girl].'

Sam Friend, the source of many of the sayings above, good-humouredly teasing his wife with a visitor: 'I married her when she was in her fair bloom, and I got to stick with her now she's an owd stalk!'

DOMESTIC SERVICE

Recollections of Winifred Spence

'I was cook-general, I suppose they call themselves now. My employers were independent people. While I was with them I started my day at six o'clock in the morning. I was very nervous when I first went; but I soon got used to it. There was a very nice housemaid when I first went. But she married and my sister took her place. I got on very well and I liked being there.

'I had the kitchen stove which was nothing but steel: I had to do that down every morning till you could see yourself in it; and whiten the hearth. I polished the steel with bath-brick; and I also had to do the morning-room stove. And that was all copper, and I had to clean that every morning with a kind of paste; and to do all the stairs and landings, and the rooms downstairs. And then, at half past eight, we used to have to get everything ready for breakfast and have it all ready; and then we had to go in for prayers. Then I cooked the breakfast. The master read the prayers (there were only two of us with the family now); and I well remember one incident. The housemaid said to me that the daughter and son-in-law were coming down for Easter (I've often had a laugh over this); and she said:

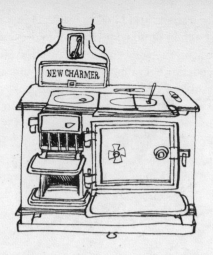

'"Oh, he's a good-looking man! He *really is* a good-looking man!"

'Well, when we went in to prayers, I burst out laughing: I never saw anyone so ugly. And of course I had to go on the carpet about that, for laughing. Yes, and they asked me what I was laughing at; and of course I couldn't say their son-in-law was so ugly, so I said:

'"Well, the housemaid said something to me before I came into prayers, and that just tickled me and I couldn't help it."

'So I got away with that all right.

'After we came out of prayers we had our breakfast, and went upstairs to make the beds and do the bedrooms. I used to help the housemaid to do that. I used to get on with the washing-up, see about the dinner and all the rest of the things. Monday morning was the laundry morning. On Monday we done all the washing. Nothing went to the laundry; and we had no one to help us – just me and the housemaid. We dried it outside; we had a nice little laundry place. You could dry it in there in wet weather. The housemaid did any repairs, the needlework that wanted doing: that was the housemaid's job.

'We could have a rest in the afternoons, if we had time. Sometimes we had; sometimes we hadn't. We had an afternoon and evening once a week; and I had to be in at nine, not a minute later. And every other Sunday, afternoon and evening off; and the next Sunday, the morning to go to church. And we had our money once a quarter: half a crown a week. Then I had to save up and buy myself a black dress for the afternoons when the housemaid was out, you see. It took me quite a long time. We had to supply our own clothes: caps and aprons. Oh yes! caps and aprons. Oh yes! and stiff collars. I can't think what we looked like then! They always had dinner at night, about seven. They kept a lot of company. They always had somebody staying there; and we used to get into bed about ten o'clock – later than that sometimes when they had a dinner party! Still, I was happy there.'

Annie Cable

'It was a tiring job. I've gone to bed many and many a time – and I was only sixteen – I've gone to bed many a time and laid on the bed and fell off to sleep before I was undressed because we were on the go the whole time. We used to have to get up at six and scrub out the still-room every morning. Very very particular they were. A beautiful house! Mind you, there was a lot of us, but still we did have to work long hours. And, of course, when we had a shooting-party, it was more like midnight before we went to bed. And I used to get round the head-one of the gardeners. He used to come in and do the flowers, all in the dining-room before the dinner was served; and it used to look glorious. Then quietly the butler would give us the down; and we used to slip in the stairs and look over the banisters and see all the ladies going into the dining-room – which was a great thrill. The still-room people and the kitchen people never came in contact with the gentry, you see.

'He [Lord Rendlesham] used to have his own coffee – I suppose you would call them plantations, would you? But we used to have the beans come over green from France. We had to roast all them and then grind all our own coffee. And it used to be a most gorgeous smell. You can imagine when we used to go to Ipswich, to Limmers' there. They used to do it. And often I would think of Rendlesham Hall. He must have been a monied gentleman because it was a marvellous house. We had an excellent living. In the summer-time we used to have the whole rib of beef, cold with salad every Sunday; our joint was that. And all of us had to assemble in the servants' hall for lunch. In the winter we used to have it hot with Yorkshire pudding. Many a time I said to my husband:

"What would I give now to have a joint of beef like I had in those days!"

'I can always remember once, the head footman coming in once for the the tea-tray. Us still-room people done all the tea. The kitchen people done breakfast, lunch and dinner at night. We always done all the tea, the cakes and everything. Well, this afternoon the tall housemaids were then going by to have their tea (they had their own sitting-room, the housemaids did); they came down the stairs. So I happened to say to the footman, I say:

'"Why can't I be like some of them girls!"

'He say: "Look . . ."

'"Some of them are nearly six foot," I said, "And here I am, very small, very short," and I was very slim in those days.

'He said: "My dear! You don't want to worry," he says. "All men admire the big ones, but they *love* the little ones!"

'So I said: "That's a little bit o' comfort I get then for being small!"

'I was there at Rendlesham Hall just over two years; and then I went to Viscount Harcourt at Newnham Park, Oxfordshire. Oh! that really was a most marvellous place. I used to help make their household bread: two hundred loaves at the time, three times a week. We made all our own bread. There was a tremendous big staff there. There was the nursery, the school-room, and the drawing-room: there were three lots. And they used to come and give us the pattern, what the butler got to lay on the table; the tea-service would be the same pattern as the tablecloth was. Of course, we had – King Edward VII came down there. I was still under-housemaid, because you had to be very clever to be a head housemaid or head still-room maid; and I said:

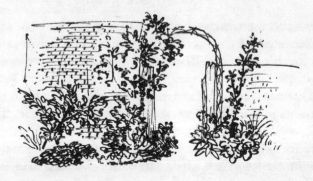

"You'll let me make the cakes?" (I was getting quite good then, although I say it myself) and I said: "Now the King is here. So I really can say I've been *Cake-Maker to the King*!

'Yes, I made a cake for Edward VII. Whether he eat any of it I don't know! But listen! The footmen there had to powder their faces, they did, really! And wear gloves. Gloves! And they used to bring us girls chocolates; because when they were coming out of the dining-room, anything nice (they hadn't time to take off their gloves) anything nice that was left in the dishes they used to pinch a piece and eat it. And the finger and thumb had always got stained, you see. So us girls used to wash their gloves out for them; and they used to buy us chocolates.'

Happy Sturgeon

'I worked for Charles Laughton, the actor, and his wife Elsa Lanchester, the actress. They lived in Gordon Square, and were on the fringe of the Bloomsbury set. There were two of us: Nellie, the cook, and me. We lived in a maisonette – the top three floors; and the bottom three floors were offices. All the servants in the Square knew one another; and Nellie, the cook that worked with me, knew Lottie – Clive Bell's cook; she was very friendly with her; and we used to go over there if they had any luncheons. Clive Bell, Mrs Bell – Vanessa Bell, Virginia

Woolf, Lady Violet Bonham-Carter, no not Lytton Strachey, John Strachey, Leonard Woolf, and Maynard Keynes, he was often there. Lord . . . he was the most famous of the lot . . . why can't I remember his name: Lord Russell! Bertrand Russell. And, of course, that was something so different for me because they treated you like one of themselves. No cap, no apron or anything. No *Sir* or *Madam*; and this was marvellous! You did your work, and there you are! No waiting at table.

'We knew all these people, and they talked to you using your Christian name. And they would talk to you – you know, as if you could read and write. And they had discussions with you. Now that was lovely, that was! I can remember Virginia Woolf at dinner parties and that. But Nellie who was with me, she'd been her cook: Nellie Boxall. She worked for her for eighteen years. But she had to leave because she was a bit highly strung; and of course you know Virginia herself was. Oh, she was lovely – she was always, sort of the grand lady. And her sister, too; we used to go round to theirs for parties. Clive Bell's wife, Vanessa, and Duncan Grant: they had a studio in Fitzroy Street. And when they had a party, Lottie, who was Clive Bell's cook – well, she did everything for him – she'd say: "There's a party round Fitzroy Street!"

'So we used to go round. Heaven knows who we used to see at the Fitzroy Street parties: we didn't know half the people that were there: we only knew the family. That's at Mrs Bell's parties – Mr Bell didn't use to go. Mrs Bell and Duncan Grant, they shared a studio; they used to live together at Fitzroy Street. They used to have exhibitions of their pupils' work; and we went there to help Lottie and showed people in, and we'd put little pinnies on to start with. We'd dress up in our party things; just put a little pinny on to start; unpack the things from Fortnum's, put them on to plates. And as soon as Mrs Bell went to bed – she used to retire quite early – there you are! We were at the party.

'The first time I ever saw Bertrand Russell he came in – this was a party at the Bells' house. And I was downstairs with Lottie; and

[177]

we were taking coats, do you see; people were coming in to lunch or dinner – I forget – we were taking the coats, and a man went upstairs – I don't know who he was – and he had a big head, and it was completely bald! The next person to come in was Bertrand Russell. And Lottie slapped him on his back and said:

'"Do you know what! There's a man just gone upstairs, and he's got a head like a bladder of lard!"

'Russell laughed, and we all laughed: she knew him as well as that. They would talk to you about things. You had an opinion. You *could* have an opinion about things. They would ask:

'"What do you think about so-and-so?" and I would say:

'"What does it matter what I think?"

'"Of course it matters!" they'd say: "You've got an opinion like everyone else!"'

COAL MINING

Miners and mining

My first introduction to the idea of collecting oral evidence was in the early 1930s. This was in the mining valleys of Glamorgan where I was born and brought up. I had graduated in 1930 and I left university in the following year, a few weeks before the economic collapse.

My immediate neighbours were miners; and in my walks on the hills, eating up time and taking the free air, I had often met groups of miners going along the old Roman road that ran along the spine of the hill above my home. If there was a cool breeze I would sometimes find them squatting on the lee side of a dry-stone wall. Here, almost any topic under the sun was likely to be tossed about in the course of a morning's talk. Sometimes there were only a couple of men 'up on the mountain'; sometimes there were as many as half a dozen sheltering under the wall. Some were unemployed, some disabled by pneumoconiosis (collier's lung); and one or two were still working, but on the night-shift which left their morning or afternoon free. I recall the occasional sunny day when the stone wall became warm with a welcome heat, and the talk was lightened by a dry humour and saving bursts of laughter. But as I look back, most of the days

were grey, with the surrounding hills withdrawn, inscrutable presences, the silence broken by the plaintive bleating of sheep, or their scuffling and sudden bedraggled appearances out of the mist.

The state of the nation was inevitably one of the major themes of the talk on the hills at that period; but so also was the change that was taking place rapidly in the collieries of the steam-coal areas where work was being 'rationalized', a much-used euphemism for the cutting of labour costs. Although ventilation of the mines (by huge steam-driven fans) and haulage (the raising and lowering of the cage or lift in the deep mines, and much of the transport underground) had long been mechanized, work at the actual coal-face was still done by hand in many collieries; and pit-ponies still dragged the small four-wheeled *drams* – the tubs or trams from the working places to link up with the mechanized 'journeys'. Up to this period, mining had been essentially a hand-craft where, as in farming, man-power and horse-power had been the chief means of winning the product. This hand-craft stage was characterized by the *stall system.* In the stall method of working, a collier and his helper – the boy – worked a limited space of the coal-face with the old hand-tools: the mandril or pick, the shovel, the hand boring-set and the axe for cutting the timber that supported the roof. Now, the mechanical coal-cutter, the conveyor belt, and the steel arch for roof support were quickly supplanting the old hand-methods, and for the stalls were substituting the long face where the coal-cutter undercut a greater length of the coal-seam, and the colliers, instead of working in pairs, now worked in groups, filling the coal on to the moving conveyor belt that ran parallel to the face.

Going underground

Mining remained a craft until the early part of the last war, with each collier taking a boy as a kind of 'apprentice' into his stall; and in some instances trying him out later with another boy, both under supervision in an adjacent stall, until they could prove themselves to be master-craftsmen, able to work the stall and be trusted to look after themselves. But sometimes before going underground a boy, on leaving school, went to work on the *screens* which were on the surface – *top-pit*. Here the coal that was brought up from underground was tipped on to a slow-moving endless belt: the boys, standing alongside, took off the slag or rubbish that was mixed with the coal. After *screening* for some months on the surface of the mine, a boy would then link up with a collier who would take him as help mate or *butty* in his stall. Often a boy's father was the first to take him below. Hywel Jeffreys (Jeff Camnant) described his first day underground:

'I started work at Christmas-time in Banwen colliery, the 29th of December. It was a Saturday. I had to go to sign on; and I had to show my birth certificate. After I signed, the manager told me that I'd remember that date for the rest of my life. So far he hasn't been wrong! And I was walking down with my *yorks* [straps below the knee] and my belt, everything tied and dressed

properly like a collier. After we went down about a hundred yards, we had to take a spell for me to get used to the darkness underground because the small flame of the oil-lamp wasn't showing enough light. Five or ten minutes by there, and getting introduced to all the old colliers that were in the same *manhole*, that we called it: I started down then to follow my father; and I had to follow him like a little dog, all the way. And it was rough going, and I had to watch my head and I had to watch where I was putting my feet. Down a steep *hard-heading*, that is a part of the drift driven from one seam to another through a *fault*. And I went down a few hundred yards again. Then we met the firemen that were coming back to meet us – the firemen of the district where I was supposed to work. They were glad to see me and they shook me by the hand and one of them said:

' *"Mae dy hâf bach di wedi passo! Mae'n rhaid iti weithio nawr."* '

[Your summer is over; and now you must go to work.]

Having your lamp

'But I looked forward to going down the mine. Yes; and that's what it was; a badge of manhood; because you sensed *that* before you went into the mine, because you were wearing the moleskin trousers. It couldn't come quick enough! I went, as I said, on the 8th of January 1918, me and two other chaps (the two have gone now, passed on now), starting the same day. *Having our lamps*, they used to call it. "You're having your lamp on the 8th of January." The old Davey safety lamp.'

JOHN WILLIAMS

Victimization

One aspect of the organization underground has not been touched on directly; that is the pressure on individuals either by the management or the owners to comply with their interpretation of the order of things. The blanket term used by the men was *victimization*. It took many forms. John Williams who became a colliery manager in 1934, and later manager of the Banwen colliery under the National Coal Board, described how as a young man he had an early glimpse of one kind of *persuasion*:

'I was an agitator – or whatever you call it: I was leading the boys, and the younger miners after that. And an old official told me:

'"I want to have a few words with you, John. Now you've passed your fireman's certificate; but a certificate is no good to you unless you got a job! And going on as you are, you won't get a job as a fireman."

'"Well, what about it?"

'"Well, if you went for the certificate you want the job, don't you?"

'"I didn't say that!" and I hinted that my father wanted me to go into the pulpit, and there was a little clash between us.

'"No!" he said, "you'll never get a job as long as your father is taking the *Daily Herald*!"

'That is a fact. That was in the twenties – 1927. And I was told I would never get a job as a fireman. And I never did have. Never did have it!

' "Because you got to learn," they said. "You've got to learn. You've got to behave."

A mining disaster

Alfred Adler suggested that a man's earliest memories give a clue to his temperament and so, by implication, to the course of his later life. If this is so, some of my earliest memories heralded a life full of gloom and disaster, or at best, a consuming interest in the spectacular, even the morbid. One memory is very clear: that of the biggest disaster in British mining history. It happened in 1913 at Senghenydd in mid-Glamorgan, a mining village just over the hill and the moorland a few miles from my home. I recall clearly the photograph of the pit-head that appeared in the newspaper next day; but the impression etched indelibly into my four-year-old mind was the sight I beheld on the Sunday following. Our house backed on to Cefn Leyshon, part of the ridge of Mynydd Eglwysilian that separated us from Senghenydd. Hundreds of miners from the western valleys were walking over the hill to the stricken village. They wore their Sunday black and were climbing along the path over the hill, girding it as if with an emblematic mourning ribbon.

Boyhood in Abercynon

Keeping a shop during the war was an arduous business. We opened at 9 a.m. and closed between 7 and 8 p.m. On Fridays and Saturdays businesses were open until midnight. From quite an early age I was expected to be somewhere around. One of my first jobs in the morning, when I was not at school, was to sweep out the customers' part of the shop. First I sprinkled the floor with water to prevent the dust from rising as I swept it. Then I got a hand bowl full of fresh sawdust from a sack in the little warehouse and sprinkled it on the clean boards. Next I had to run errands and to do various little jobs like drawing a pint of vinegar from a big barrel in the warehouse or sawing up blocks of salt with a special saw into a prescribed thickness, ready to be packed in brown paper. Later in the war, when sugar was very strictly rationed, we had a big barrel of molasses, a thick syrup, in the small warehouse. We could draw off a pint to fill a customer's empty jam jar.

Above the warehouse was the storeroom where there were shelves holding brightly coloured tin canisters decorated with Indian and Chinese letters. Here was also a coffee machine in which we ground the beans when a customer wanted freshly ground coffee. In the storeroom was also the cheese rack. The Caerphilly cheeses were made in Penywaun farm which was only three or four miles from Caerphilly itself. Father bought the cheeses on a counter-account with Mrs Thomas: he took the cheeses she made and supplied her with the equivalent value of goods and animal foods. When the cheeses came from the farm they had been taken fresh from the moulds. They were placed in the wooden rack to mature and acquire a skin or rind. The round cheeses were about eight inches in diameter and about two inches thick. They stood on their ends in the inward sloping shelves for a fortnight or so when they came in during the spring or early summer.

Hill farms

Most of my early excursions were official journeys to the farms on the hills. I went with Father or my brother Jack at first, but later I took the horse and cart up myself. If I went with Jack, I got out of the cart at the steep climb out of the valley and walked up a grassy path to avoid the loop of the ascending road along which Jack led the horse and cart. Once we were on the fairly flat back of the hill, I clambered back into the cart and we were away past the farms, Y Llechwen, Y Garth Fawr, Y Garth Fach through winding lanes bordered by low stone walls. Farther beyond Llechwan was a farm kept by Mr Miles. On an early visit there, my father stopped to call on his old friend and he left my younger brother Roy and me in the trap. While he was inside one of the farmer's daughters brought out a couple of glasses of milk for us. Roy, who was about four and hadn't been used to drinking out of a glass, took a bite at his and broke a chunk out of it.

The visits to the hill farms were the highlights of our days and from an early age I peopled them in my imagination with a different class of being. There was a hollow, not far from the Miles farm, called Pant y Ddawns (The Hollow of the Dance) which fairies were supposed to frequent and were actually seen by some people. Another small farm was shown me as the place where the mother of a young baby had forgotten to place the poker over its cradle: as a consequence the child, unprotected by iron, had been stolen by the fairies and replaced by a 'changeling'. I was young enough to believe these tales implicitly, but my early sense of wonder in the hills has never entirely vanished.

We often visited Penywaun, a big farm near the highest point of the 'mountain', as we invariably called the hills when we were young. Mr Thomas Penywaun was one of my father's first customers at the shop and he became a firm friend. But he died rather young, leaving his widow to carry on the farm and bring up their three children. Mrs Thomas always made us welcome, whether we were delivering goods or taking a pleasure trip in the trap. As soon as we arrived after our long pull from the valley, she would arrange to have the horse taken out of the shafts. A farm-worker who lived in the house would stable him and give him water and a handful of hay.

Mrs Thomas was the model of the traditional hospitality of the old hill community: whoever called it was a point of honour to welcome them. She was a very efficient, neat woman with a reddish face, her hair parted in the middle and drawn back tightly against her head. She rarely smiled but this was not through a lack of good nature: her responsibilities had given her a serious expression. As soon as she helped the maid to clear the table, we had our feet under it, after first washing our hands.

The table was a very long one, with bare scrubbed boards; there were no chairs, only benches. There was always a full company of farm-workers, maids and visitors. It was always a high-tea with toasted cheese, homemade bread and butter, and *bara brith* loaves that were sweetened by dried fruit, literally 'speckled bread'.

I did not recognize the Evans family of Penygraig as some of the last members of the old immemorial community of the hills until I had talked with Edward Thomas of Penywaun. I had seen them with the eyes of a young boy, but Edward who knew them well was able to interpret them with the mind of a man. At Penywaun, years later, he told me about John Evans and his sister as they were at the first two decades of this century: I sensed as a boy they were unusual but now I recognized how different they were. John Evans the farmer did not buy a *gambo*, the traditional farm-cart of Glamorgan, until 1902 or 1903. He paid £4.10s.0d. for a secondhand one at a sale. Previously the only vehicle he had was a *car llusg* – a slide-car, one of the most primitive vehicles used in animal traction. It had no wheels and the horse was harnessed to two long shafts that he dragged along the ground. The load was fixed across the poles of shafts by means of a wicker basket or a wooden container made to fit horizontally on the sloping shafts. The slide-car was as old as history yet it had one advantage: the farmer could carry loads on gradients where it would be dangerous to take a wheeled cart. Yet the contrast that presented itself to me as Edward Thomas described it was dramatic: down in the valley less than half a mile away was a modern colliery with all the latest gadgetry of modern technology, while the hill farmers (at least some of them) were still in the Middle Ages – even earlier, as far as their material culture was concerned.

Welsh magic

One of the most attractive features of the Glamorgan hill landscape is the whitewashed farmhouses: *muriau gwynion Morganwg* (the white walls of Glamorgan) were celebrated in medieval Welsh poetry; and even today they can still be seen glinting in the spring sunshine. They fit the Glamorgan scene perfectly. But the people who built them are likely to have had other preoccupations besides natural beauty: one of these was the unseen life that went on around them – good and evil. It was against the evil influences that they had to take precautions; and white was one of their defences against them, their first assurance – as in other parts of the world – a sure bulwark to the place where they were to spend most of their days.

A WRITER'S MEMORIES

A meeting

I had a day off from the aerodrome and went by camp bus to the town of Ayr, returning by an ordinary service bus in the mid-evening. The bus went on to the town of Govan and dropped me on the main road, to walk down the hill to the camp that was about a mile away on a gentle descent. A young girl got off the bus at the same time. She wore WAAF uniform and we walked down to the camp together. She was a wireless operator in the station headquarters – in signals, the same trade as I was in. She came from the Isle of Lewis, and had the dark colouring of the people of the islands and a pensive air, the inwardness that marks off some of the women of the west coast and the islands. As soon as we came in sight of the sea, we saw a beautiful sunset; stretched out below us was the whole scene even more spectacular than it appeared from the shore. We stopped for a moment or two and stood in silence. Then we walked on, admiring the scene spread out below us. Then she said quietly as though communing with herself and not addressing a remark to me: 'And I've promised to marry an Englishman!'

Darcher's dicky

Buying the playing field was a major undertaking for a small village. Yet the people were very spirited and rallied together to organize various projects to raise the money. One of the most successful efforts was the adapting of the marl-pit to stage an open-air play. It required little shaping, simply the cutting down of the vegetation with which it was overgrown and a levelling of its floor for an auditorium. On one side there was a mound of earth that was covered with grass. It formed a perfect, natural stage. By the side of this the shrubs had been left to form a 'green room' where the actors could wait to go on to the stage. A very good amateur company from Ipswich volunteered to come out and give a performance. The play chose itself: *A Midsummer Night's Dream.* We got an extension from the mains of the newly won electricity and we borrowed floodlights. The evening was a fine one in June and the play was an outstanding success. Most of the older villagers had never seen a full-length play before, certainly not by Shakespeare, and they enjoyed the novelty enormously. They identified with 'the hempen homespuns' especially as they spoke in broad Suffolk The high spot for the Blaxhall part of the audience was the first appearance of the 'translated' Bottom. One of them called out: 'My heart alive! Here comes Darcher's dicky.' Darcher Poacher was the man who formerly carted marl from the pit with his cart and his dicky was the donkey.

Blackhall: Robert Savage's cottage

Robert and Priscilla Savage

It was a piece of good fortune that I had Robert Savage as my neighbour. He ... spent a lot of time gardening and tending his pigs, which he kept in a yard opposite the school. They had a large family who had all left home except their eldest son, Willy, who was deaf and dumb. It was one of the children's delights to watch him or his father feeding the pigs. My contact with the Savages increased and I used to take my two charges to visit them when we were on our outings; they enjoyed watching the feeding of the ducks and the chickens. Robert Savage spoke a pure Suffolk dialect, and it was this that first alerted me to the historic wealth that was in this small village. He came from a long line of shepherds on his mother's as well as his father's side; and I recognized that many of the words he was using were centuries old, although most of them were obsolete in ordinary language. Many of them were technical words connected with the tending of sheep, and therefore had stayed alive; for the tending of sheep had not changed appreciably since the Middle Ages. Many of the words I knew through a reading of the sixteenth-century English poets, and I got a pleasurable shock through hearing them spoken by a man who took them for granted and used them as if they are a natural part of his heritage – as indeed they were.

He spoke of the time when he was a 'page' to a shepherd, and brought to light the medieval order where page was the first step in the hierarchy. He used the word 'tempest', the first time I had heard the word in ordinary conversation – apart from its use in poetry or hymns. It was in its old, particular usage of a violent thunderstorm. He said: 'There's a tempest coming up the river' – the Alde estuary, hinting that an electrical storm always follows the water. He used the word 'things' in its old meaning of animals: 'Things hoolly like the grains from the Maltings'. It was the rhythm and colour of the speech that I admired: 'I went to feed the pigs, and there was a cloud no bigger than a load of hay over towards Sherwood's. And I was a-coming back it just blacked out and down it come. I was whoolly drenched!' or again: 'Willie now got the gilt [a splayed sow] and it's a cosset [a young pig brought up by hand]. But it's settled down. Willie coached it and cosseted it, and he went and lay down with it. And now's it's all right.' I once heard Mrs Savage telling her husband when she found the cat had misbehaved itself: 'Throw the mucky owd cat abroad!' using the archaic meaning of the phrase – out of doors. 'Squat' was another ancient word she was fond of using: 'He knows it all, you may depend. But he's the

one to keep it squat,' that is, hidden or secret. Although he had been a shepherd for all of his life there was no technical query about what happened on the arable farm that he could not answer. He was my mentor as I was finding my way about the dialect terms. I discovered later that most of the words he told me were in Thomas Tusser's *Five Hundred Points of Good Husbandry*. He knew them in what, I am sure, was their original pronunciation; and he took me through the arable year and the niceties of the fallows and the rotation of the crops, pointing out in connection with the rotation that the shepherd had a good say in what crops the farmer grew. The shepherd advised him what crops he would want for his sheep and it would be a rash farmer who would ignore his shepherd's counsel. One day he was describing to me a particular form of plough share and I was making heavy weather of his explanation when he said: 'Give me your notebook for a moment: I'll make a draught [drawing] of it.'

The death of the shepherd

As time went on I saw that Robert Savage's walks past the school to tend his pigs got less frequent. His rheumatism – the bane of the shepherd's old age – got more and more crippling. He spent most of the day in his old Windsor chair in the living-room. He sat there day after day while Priscilla did her chores. He had a thrush as a companion. It would light on a bush just by the window and call his attention by its singing. He got great delight from this bird, sometimes calling out to his wife in the kitchen: 'Can you hear ma lil' owd bud, Mother? He's a-going some fine this morning.' Latterly, one of the family had bought him a budgerigar and he had the cage not far from his chair; and he talked to the bird as though it was a member of the family. Our two young daughters had a good deal of enjoyment visiting Robert Savage, to hear the bird and watch its antics. We visited him on the last day he was alive. He had been off-colour all the week and he lay in his bed that had been brought downstairs in the room next to the living-room. I went in the room to have a word with him and then went to talk to his wife who was in the next room with the two girls. Presently his wife heard a movement and went to see whether he wanted anything. She called me immediately. Robert was having a heart attack. He had raised himself and sat on the edge of his bed, probably in an attempt to ease the pain. We laid him down; and it was all over in a few seconds. There was nothing we could do. The old lady was expecting it and was quite composed. I asked her whether I should call a neighbour who was often in demand on these occasions. She said: 'I'll not have anyone lay a hand upon him!' I told her I would ring Dr Keer, and I went back to the next room and sent the girls home telling them I would soon follow them. Mary, who was seven at the time, said to me with wide eyes as they left: 'The bird has stopped singing!'

I was fond of Robert Savage, and would always be grateful to him for he was the first to communicate to me the feel of the old community of which he was a sterling member. He was my interpreter (although he was not aware of his function) of a large tract of history that for me before I met him had remained unquickened. He it was who gave me entry to what was a foreign country that, without his help, I would never have known. Later, after the funeral, Priscilla Savage told me that the thrush that sang outside the cottage went away after Robert's death: 'The day he died, it sang – oh it did sing; and he said to me: "Can you hear my babe?" I've heard that they even follow to the church-yard and sing there. Strange, isn't it?'

ORAL HISTORY

The oral tradition

The value therefore of oral evidence in a rural area like East Anglia is very high. But the question may well be put at this stage: 'Are you then saying that an unlettered countryman can inform a scientist who has devoted a lifetime specially to his subject?' The question would expose the questioner. For what he would be doing would be to confuse two different kinds of knowledge acquired in entirely different ways; and they are not in their essence antagonistic but complementary. It is not simply that one is practical and the other theoretical; for the scientist certainly puts his theories to the acid test of practice. He does this repeatedly but – and this is the important consideration – not over a sufficiently long period, as often transpires with regard to man himself and the soil on which he lives directly or indirectly. The main difference is this: although the countryman has no knowledge at all of the physics of soil structure or little of the chemistry of soil composition, the knowledge he does have has been tested in the extended social laboratory that – at least in farming in this particular region – has [come down from the Neolithic period]. His knowledge is not a personal knowledge but has been available to him through oral tradition which is the unselfconscious medium of transmission. It is in his bones, you could say, not demonstrable in a logical way but there as an insight, an intuition, and none the less valuable for that.

The components of history

We eventually moved from Blaxhall when my wife was offered a bigger school at Needham Market, a few miles farther east, a small town by East Anglian standards. I left the village with mixed feelings because I sensed that it was there I had found my life's work, although I did not fully realize this at the time. It was only some years after I left that I identified the village as my second academy when I began to learn the technique of what later became known as oral history. But more importantly, I had then an experience which sank in gradually and imperceptibly as though it was a natural growth from the environment. It was undramatic and ordinary, and hardly to be remarked upon in detail, in the then subjectively eventful course of my life. It was here at this time, and with the dressing and elaborating on it later, that I transposed the Blaxhall community in my own mind into its true place in an ancient historical sequence, keeping the continuity that was for ever changing, and for ever remaining the same, until an irreparable break substituted the machines for animal power, and put an end to a period that had lasted well over two thousand years. Yet I learned from this experience that the main components of history are not things but people. This is to make a song of a discovery of the obvious; but it is something that needs to be repeated now, especially at this time of wonderfully ingenious discoveries and inventions that have cascaded on people in an embarrassment of rich promises.

BIBLIOGRAPHY

Works by George Ewart Evans

Modern Welsh Poetry, edited by Keidrych Rhys, Faber, 1944. Contains three
poems: 'At the Seaside', 'Progress in the Peaceable Blue', 'Winter 1939'.
The Voices of the Children, Penmark Press, 1947.
Ask the Fellows Who Cut the Hay, Faber, 1956.
Welsh Short Stories, edited by George Ewart Evans, Faber, 1959, second
edition. Contains his own story *The Medal*.
The Horse in the Furrow, Faber, 1960.
The Pattern Under the Plough: Aspects of the Folk-Life of East Anglia, Faber,
1966.
The Farm and the Village, Faber, 1969.
Where Beards Wag All: The Relevance of the Oral Tradition, Faber, 1970.
The Leaping Hare by George Ewart Evans and David Thomson, Faber,
1972.
Acky, Faber, 1973.
The Days That We Have Seen, Faber, 1975.
Let Dogs Delight and Other Stories, Faber, 1975.
From Mouths of Men, Faber, 1976.
Horse Power and Magic, Faber, 1979.
The Strength of the Hills: An Autobiography, Faber, 1983.
Spoken History, Faber, 1987.

SOURCES